FROM TRAGEDY TO TRIUMPH

FROM TRAGEDY TO TRIUMPH

The Message of the Book of Job

By

H. L. ELLISON, B.A., B.D.

Wm. B. Eerdmans Publishing Company
Grand Rapids, Michigan

This American Edition
is published by arrangement with
The Paternoster Press, London

Library of Congress Catalog No. 58–9553

MADE AND PRINTED IN GREAT BRITAIN

To my Friends
ISAAC and LYDIA FEINSTEIN
who have shown me,
one in death,
the other in life,
how to suffer to the glory of
God

CONTENTS

PREFACE

I UNDERTOOK the obligation to furnish a series of studies on the Book of Job to *The Hebrew Christian Quarterly* something more than three years ago. I had hardly started my task, when a period of suffering and distress broke over me, which profoundly affected my understanding of the book and the scale of my treatment of it. These studies have now been thoroughly revised and considerably expanded.

There are few books of the Bible more difficult to write on than Job. One may, on the one hand, give one's interpretation of the thought but entirely lose touch with the actual text in so doing. On the other hand one may so occupy oneself with the difficulties of the language that the spiritual message and the poetry become swamped under textual and linguistic comments. However much my exposition may have dressed itself in modern clothes, I have always tried to see to it that it does not stray far from the text; since poetry is as much understood by the heart as by the brain, I have not troubled overmuch about minor difficulties in the R.V. —the A.V. is generally only then mentioned, when there was need to warn against its rendering—when I thought that the general meaning was clear.

The main writings on *Job* I have leaned on will be found by referring to the list of abbreviations. My thanks are due to Messrs. Burns & Oates for their gracious permission to quote Monsignor Ronald Knox's translation of 12: 13–25 as well as of odd verses elsewhere. The text printed at the beginning of chapters or sections is that of the R.V., with the substitution of the marginal renderings, when these are generally accepted as superior.

My hope is that just as Job's anguish brought me comfort in the days of my distress, so this book will make the triumph of Job more real and a greater blessing to others who pass through distress.

H. L. ELLISON.

LIST OF ABBREVIATIONS

This work uses standard abbreviations for the names of the books of the Bible as well as many in common use. Only the following need mention.

a (b, c)	refers to the first (second or third) part of the verse mentioned.
ad loc.	at the appropriate place.
A.V.	The Authorised or King James' Version of 1611.
Davidson	Davidson & Lanchester: *The Book of Job*—Cambridge Bible for Schools and Colleges, edition of 1918.
f.	and the following verse.
ff.	and the following two verses.
I.C.C.	Driver & Gray: *The Book of Job*—International Critical Commentary (1921).
Job	The Book of Job in contrast to the man.
Koehler	Koehler & Baumgartner: *Lexicon in Veteris Testamenti Liberos*.
Knox	Bible translation by Monsignor Knox; O.T. in 1949.
mg.	margin.
Moffatt	Bible translation by James Moffatt; O.T. in 1924.
Peake	Peake: *Job*—The Century Bible (1905).
R.S.V.	Revised Standard Version; O.T. in 1952.
R.V.	Revised Version; O.T. in 1885.
Stevenson	Stevenson: *The Poem of Job*—The Schweich Lectures for 1943.
Strahan	Strahan: *The Book of Job* (1914).
tx.	text.

THE STRUCTURE OF JOB

A.   Prologue in Heaven and on Earth, chs. 1, 2
B.   Job's Complaint, ch. 3
C.   Job's Friends, chs. 4–27

    1. First Cycle of Discussion, chs. 4–14
        (*a*) Eliphaz, chs. 4, 5
        (*b*) Job replies, chs. 6, 7
        (*c*) Bildad, ch. 8
        (*d*) Job replies, chs. 9, 10
        (*e*) Zophar, ch. 11
        (*f*) Job replies, chs. 12–14

    2. Second Cycle of Discussion, chs. 15–21
        (*a*) Eliphaz, ch. 15
        (*b*) Job replies, chs. 16, 17
        (*c*) Bildad, ch. 18
        (*d*) Job replies, ch. 19
        (*e*) Zophar, ch. 20
        (*f*) Job replies, ch. 21

    3. Third Cycle of Discussion, chs. 22–27
        (*a*) Eliphaz, ch. 22
        (*b*) Job replies, chs. 23, 24
        (*c*) Bildad, ch. 25
        (*d*) Job replies, chs. 26, 27*

D.   Interlude: In Praise of Wisdom, ch. 28
E.   Job's Summing Up, chs. 29–31
    1. The Past, ch. 29
    2. The Present, ch. 30
    3. The Future, ch. 31

F.   Elihu's Interruption, chs. 32–37
    1. Introduction, ch. 32
    2. First Answer, ch. 33
    3. Second Answer, ch. 34
    4. Third Answer, chs. 35–37

G.   God's Reply, chs. 38–42: 6
H.   Epilogue on Earth, ch. 42: 7–17

* But see pages 21 and 87 f.

CHAPTER I

THE BOOK OF JOB

MANY who have never read *Job* have caught something of its spirit as they have listened to the Burial Service of *The Book of Common Prayer*. Three times *Job* is quoted:

The Lord gave, and the Lord hath taken away; blessed be the Name of the Lord (1: 21),

and,

Man that is born of a woman hath but a short time to live, and is full of misery. He cometh up, and is cut down, like a flower; he fleeth as it were a shadow, and never continueth in one stay (14: 1f);

there is also the triumphant note taken up as well in Handel's *Messiah*,

I know that my Redeemer liveth, and that he shall stand at the latter day upon the earth. And though after my skin worms destroy this body, yet in my flesh shall I see God: whom I shall see for myself, and my eyes shall behold, and not another (19: 25ff).

Great writers and theologians have hailed it as a poetic masterpiece. Carlyle's words may serve as an example*:

I call it, apart from all theories about it, one of the grandest things ever written with pen. One feels, indeed, as if it were not Hebrew; such a noble universality, different from noble patriotism or noble sectarianism, reigns in it. A noble Book; all men's Book! It is our first, oldest statement of the never-ending Problem—man's destiny, and God's way with him here in this earth. And all in such free flowing outlines; grand in its sincerity, in its simplicity; in its epic melody, and repose of reconcilement . . . Sublime sorrow, sublime reconciliation; oldest choral music as of the heart of mankind;—so soft, and

* *On Heroes and Hero-Worship*, p. 49 in Centenary Edition.

great; as the summer midnight, as the world with its seas and stars! There is nothing written, I think, in the Bible or out of it, of equal literary merit.

A catena of similar opinions may be found in Strahan, p. 28f.

For maturer men and women who are familiar with the Bible there are few Old Testament stories that exercise a stronger and more perennial attraction than that of Job. This is not because of the poetry of the book, though unfortunate is the man who has not felt the music and poetic power of some of its chapters. It is not even because of the effect made on him by the book as a whole, for the number of those who have intelligently read the whole book is small. It is rather that when life loses the first simplicities of youth we increasingly feel its mysteries, that of suffering being perhaps its greatest. As the Lord leads us in strange paths of pain and loss, or when our eyes are opened to glimpse something of the anguish around us, we feel that even if we cannot understand all in the book of Job, it does indicate an answer to these problems.

There are two main reasons for the lack of detailed knowledge and understanding of *Job* among Bible students. The former derives from the fact that it is poetry of the highest order. Tennyson could say that it was "the greatest poem of ancient or modern times." The effort of mind and heart needed, if we are to enter into the depths of great poetry, is not one that most associate with the study of the Bible. The second is the inadequacy of the Authorised Version. Davidson, no mean or biased critic, says (p. lxxviii), "Of the English Versions the A.V. appears at its worst in this book. It is frequently obscure and several times it misses the meaning entirely . . . The R.V. has done much to make the book intelligible to English readers."

Though this present attempt to grasp and display the message of *Job* is based on the R.V., no more modern rendering has been despised, whether taken from a translation of the Bible or from a commentary, if it has brought out the meaning more clearly. The R.S.V. has proved especially helpful.

We may perhaps add a third and more subtle reason for our difficulty in understanding and appreciating *Job*. From Greece our civilization has learnt to think in general terms and abstract conceptions. The world of the Old Testament thought, as does the Western child today, in concrete terms and of particular cases.

We talk vaguely of the problem of suffering; the Old Testament deals with Job's 'Why?' We feel that to reach the truth we must strip a problem of its 'accidentals'; the Old Testament presents Job as a figure in the round, detailing apparently all the accidentals of his life. Closer study shows that it is wiser and more subtle than that. All that is needed to make Job a real man for the writer's generation is retained; that which would make him an alien to the reader is normally passed over, but for all that the "accidentals" are an essential part of the book.

Unfortunately, however, there is an immeasurably greater gulf between us and the writer's generation than there was between them and Job. We are in danger of being so occupied with the exotic details of life and thought in the land of Uz, details which still live on there, that we fail to realize how modern Job and his questionings, his friends and their obtuseness are. That is why so much in this exposition is devoted to stripping the characters of their Eastern garments, that they may speak to us in the language of today.

CHAPTER II

THE MODERN SCHOLAR LOOKS AT JOB

THE scholar has been attracted to *Job* just as the ordinary man has been, for the problem it handles spares no rank or class, nor can learning free us from suffering. He has, however, found additional attractions in the book, when he has looked on it merely as a literary product. Very many of the questions he has raised and discussed have no bearing on the purpose of this book and may be completely ignored. Others, however, vitally affect our understanding of *Job* and must be briefly considered.

AUTHORSHIP AND DATE

There is no agreement on the date when *Job* was written, and no convincing suggestion as to its authorship has ever been made. While it is true that the "official" Talmudic tradition (*Baba Bathra* 14b, *seq.*) attributes it to Moses, the discussion that follows it shows that it is no more than a pious pronouncement of no authority, for the rabbis place the book, or the lifetime of Job, at varying times between Isaac and Joseph to Cyrus and Ahasuerus. Virtually the only arguments that can be advanced in favour of Mosaic authorship are a general sense of fitness, and the use in common of certain rarer words in *Job* and the Pentateuch. In fact the differences of vocabulary are more striking than the similarities, and subjective arguments can be made to prove almost anything.

Both the *International Standard Bible Encyclopedia* and Young in his *Introduction to the Old Testament* reject a Mosaic authorship, and it seems clear that we should bow to the Holy Spirit's silence and accept the book as anonymous. As regards the date of the book we would do well to take up a similar position. Young adopts the view of Delitzsch that it was written in the time of Solomon, but the evidence can equally well be interpreted as supporting a later date. The simple fact is that nothing depends either on the date of composition or on the authorship.

16

The suggestion that the book must be early because the law of Moses, the Exodus, etc., are not mentioned has no validity, because the characters in it are not Israelites, and it is no chance that in the actual speeches the name Jehovah is found only once (12: 9), and here seven manuscripts, undoubtedly rightly, have God instead. The background is, in fact, kept deliberately as general and as vague as possible, so that the problem of Job may be seen in all its mystery, unobscured by any purely temporal considerations.

HISTORY OR PARABLE?

It will come as a surprise to many that there have been Jewish rabbis who denied the historicity of Job. The Talmud (*Baba Bathra* 15a) tells us of one in the third century A.D. who stated, "Job did not exist and was not created; he is a parable." While the view was obviously a minority one, Maimonides, the greatest Jewish scholar of the early middle ages, could say (*Moreh Nebuchim* iii. 22), "Its basis is a fiction, conceived for the purpose of explaining the different opinions which people held on Divine Providence." While we do not agree with this, we believe that, at least in its earlier formulation, it was intended to express a truth which most today tacitly accept.

Ezek. 14: 14, 20 is sufficient evidence for the historical existence of Job. If I am correct in earlier statements* as to the identity of the Daniel here mentioned by Ezekiel, he is referring to three men from an early date in human history. It is also clear that the story of Job circulated widely in forms differing materially from that in the Bible—a summary will be found in Stevenson, pp. 76–86—but, in spite of the opinion of Theodore, Bishop of Mopsuestia (392–428), I see no reason for preferring any of the popular versions to the form of the story in the Bible.

Though the story will have come down the centuries to the writer of the book, its heart (chs. 3–42: 6) will represent his re-writing of it under the Spirit's guidance. The difficulties of style and language prevented the translators of the A.V. from doing justice to the magnificence of the poetic language, and though the R.V. is much superior, it still leaves much to be desired. As a result we often fail to realize that we cannot be reading a verbatim report: we have a poetic transformation of the original prose narrative before us.

* *Men Spake from God*, p. 142; *Ezekiel: The Man and His Message*, p. 59.

B

Against this there has been urged the ability of the Arab to break out in spontaneous poetic utterance, when under great emotional stress. If it were only Job who speaks in poetry, we might give considerable weight to this fact, but all the characters do, and all the time at that.

This is not to suggest that *Job* is a mere invention based on an old story, or that the author has so transformed his hero that he would not have recognized himself. We have the same magic of the Spirit's transforming power as in the Psalms. There the joys and sorrows of men, David and others, are taken and so transformed that they have become expressive of the experiences of all men of God, so that the Psalter is the hymn book of Synagogue and Church alike. In the same way the sufferings and strivings of Job and the sophistications of his friends have been touched with a gold that makes them speak to all generations in all lands.

When modern Jewish scholars claim that Job is a parable of Israel and its sufferings, there is more than a little truth in it. Though Job is an individual and a historical character, he is also the representative sufferer. So too, when we pass from the individual to the national, the Jew stands before us in a representative character. Jewry, knowing the hand of God to be over it, but suffering as no other people, without knowing why, shows true spiritual insight, when it sees the parallel between itself and Job.

JOB AND WISDOM LITERATURE

Our unknown author did more than turn the prose of suffering into deathless verse and universalize it; he definitely set it in the framework of what is now known as "wisdom literature"; on this point conservative and liberal are of one mind. It links up with Proverbs and Ecclesiastes.

In an age in which the possibilities of book learning were few, those who had it were known as the Wise and were highly honoured in the community. In Jer. 18:18, we find them standing beside the priest and the prophet. As Rylaarsdam says of them "The role of the sages and the public estimate of them were very similar in all lands. They were the schoolmasters and the court counsellors."[*] Since God wills to be served by all

[*] *Revelation in Jewish Wisdom Literature*, p. 9.

portions of a man, we have the wisdom of the Wise represented in the Old Testament.

In Proverbs we see the Wise, Solomon and others, seeking to understand the working out of God's providence among men. Apart from Agur (ch. 30), they are convinced that where the fear of the Lord is there also will be an understanding of His works. They saw in man's experiences such uniformities that the Wise, if they were humble, could lay down the general methods of God's workings. Note that there is no claim to prophetic inspiration in Proverbs.

In Qohelet (Ecclesiastes) the writer, placing himself in the position of Solomon in his old age, a disappointed backslider whose unequalled wisdom had failed to make him wise in the things of God, questions the unqualified optimism of Proverbs. He shows that however great the wisdom it will fail to make sense of God's actions, if it once becomes purely self-centred.

Job, on the other hand, is a direct challenge to the whole concept of Proverbs. As we shall see in our study, one of its main conclusions is that man cannot always understand the ways of God, and God does not always will to reveal them to men. Job is finally satisfied not by having his questions answered but by a revelation of the incomparable majesty of God.

There is no real contradiction between the three wisdom books. The picture given in Proverbs holds good for the vast majority of cases. The case of Job is obviously intended to be exceptional, but we cannot dictate to God whether we are to have exceptions or not. God may at any time upset our carefully made plans and show that His actions cannot be contained within the narrow span of human understanding. Qohelet then reminds us that all our wisdom is nothing worth unless it is linked with true godliness; otherwise the purposes of God will always remain enigmatic even to the wisest. So the three books form a spiritual unity, and we may never forget the message of the other two as we study *Job*.

Earlier I said that our author had deliberately set *Job* in the framework of what is now known as "wisdom literature". This was not meant to imply that it is in any way typical of wisdom literature, as Proverbs is. Pfeiffer writes very well:*

   "If our poet ranks with the greatest writers of mankind, as can hardly be doubted, his creative genius did not of necessity rely on earlier models for the general structure of his work and

* *Introduction to the Old Testament*, p. 683f.

for the working out of its details.   Admitting at the outset that there is no close parallel to his poem, in form and substance, we may regard it as one of the most original works in the poetry of mankind.   So original in fact that it does not fit into any of the standard categories devised by literary criticism.   All general classifications fail to do justice to the overflowing abundance of its forms, moods, and thoughts; it is not exclusively lyric, . . . nor epic, . . . nor dramatic, . . . nor didactic or reflective, . . . unless the poem is cut down to fit a particular category. . . . Even the more comprehensive characterizations . . . fail to do justice to the scope of the work."

We must bear in mind also that whatever the rank and social position of Job and his friends, they are introduced to us as belonging to the Wise.   The one exception is Elihu.   Entirely consistently with this their discussions are, so far as Job will allow them to be, the discussions of the Wise, in which we see the world mirrored not always as it is but as it ideally should be. The anguished realism of Job first angers them and then silences them, but if Job is more realistic than they, it is because he has learnt from bitter experience.

The Integrity of the Book

The question whether the prose framework of *Job*, as we now have it, is by the same author as the verse that forms the heart of the book, or whether it is older, is normally a mere literary question, and as such may be ignored.   But there are cases like that of Stevenson in his recent penetrating study of the book, where the separation is made in order that the poetic part may be given an interpretation contrary to that permitted by the prose introduction.   We grant without hesitation, that by this process much of the difficulty of the book is removed, but this is an outstanding example of how the Bible must not be handled and interpreted.   No really cogent reason for the separation is given; indeed the whole suggestion is in itself most improbable.   Apart from this we are under obligation to let the Word speak to us in its wholeness, not to cut it down and cut it up until it suits our perception.

Most modern commentaries wish to delete longer or shorter parts of the book as later insertions.   The reasons given are almost invariably subjective, and they are normally palpably weak or of minor importance. The only two cases noted in this book are ch. 28, the Praise of Wisdom, and the speeches of Elihu (chs. 32–37). It has seemed wisest to defer discussion of these passages until they are reached in the normal order of events, cf. pp. 89 and 103. It is only as we have been studying *Job* through all its development of thought that we shall be in an adequate position to judge whether these passages do or do not fit into its warp and woof.

It has been very strongly urged that in places the text has been dislocated. Our increasing knowledge of ancient manuscripts shows us how easily this might have happened. The most obvious example is 31: 38ff. There can be no doubt that 31: 35ff represent the climax and conclusion of Job's words—as they stand, the closing verses of the chapter present an intolerable anticlimax. It is easier, however, to recognize the dislocation than to say at what point in the chapter the misplaced verses originally stood.

The other passage that concerns us is chs. 25–27. As our text stands, Bildad gives a half-hearted reply in ch. 25, and when Job answers in ch. 26, Zophar shrugs his shoulders and leaves Job to wind up in ch. 27. If it stood by itself, there would be no real difficulty in the fact that in 26: 5–14, Job out-Bildads Bildad in his description of God's greatness and transcendence, but in 27: 13–23, we find Job repeating his friends' views on the fate of the wicked in even stronger terms than they had used, although in 27: 5, 6, 12, he had just reaffirmed his unshakable dissent. This is patently absurd and a contradiction of the book as a whole. None of the many attempts to re-arrange the text is wholly convincing, and the trouble may be in part due to loss of a section owing to the breaking of the papyrus roll. In the treatment of the text in ch. VII no attempt at rearrangement has been made.

THE POETRY OF THE BOOK OF JOB

When we try to discover what determines whether a passage of literature is to be considered prose or poetry, we find that there are two factors involved. One, undoubtedly the more important, is the language used. This is so generally recognized, that there is no need to deal with it here. Long before the technical principles of Hebrew poetry became known to Western readers, the beauty of the language of *Job*, even in translation, had brought universal conviction that here was poetry of the highest order.

The other factor that distinguishes poetry from prose is that the former uses certain technical devices which create the sense of compactness and regularity. These have varied from period to period and language to language.

Almost the first thing that strikes a child about the poetry, or it might be better to say verse, that it meets is the rhymes. These are completely lacking in Biblical poetry, though they may be found in mediaeval or modern Hebrew poetic writings. It is true that Stevenson claims (p. 60), "Rhyme is used very sparingly, but it is not to be ignored where it occurs." This is unlikely; the few examples are probably accidental or possibly special cases of assonance. Alliteration in the formal sense in which it is normally used in English is not found either, but assonance, the repetition of similar sounds, is quite frequent in *Job*, far more so than is normal in Hebrew poetry.

The second feature in most of our poetry that strikes even the casual reader is the regular rhythm we call metre. This undoubtedly existed as a major factor in Hebrew poetry, but for various reasons we are not able to be certain of its details today. There seems little doubt, however, that more metrical freedom was allowed than in most English poetry.

To these technical devices Hebrew adds parallelism, which is unknown in classical or modern European poetry. It may be briefly explained by saying that each metrical unit was divided into two, occasionally three or even four, approximately equal sections. Normally this metrical unit, except in the prophets, coincides with the traditional verse divisions. The thought in the first section is then in some way continued or balanced in the following section, or sections.* The printing adopted in the R.V. and more modern versions, except Knox, makes this parallelism clear.

The outstanding importance of this parallelism has been that it has permitted translators to give the sense of rhythm and balance in Hebrew poetry without having to struggle to reproduce its metres and assonances. A word of warning has to be given to the reader. He must always be prepared to take the metrical unit as a whole in his interpretation instead of concentrating on the smaller sections. These are consciously incomplete.

* A more formal treatment of the subject is given in my *Men Spake from God*; reference can also be made to any good Bible dictionary.

CHAPTER III

THE PROLOGUE

THERE was a man in the land of Uz, whose name was Job; and that man was perfect and upright, and one that feared God, and eschewed evil. ²And there were born unto him seven sons and three daughters. ³His substance also was seven thousand sheep, and three thousand camels, and five hundred yoke of oxen, and five hundred she-asses, and a very great household; so that this man was the greatest of all the children of the east. ⁴And his sons went and held a feast in the house of each one upon his day; and they sent and called for their three sisters to eat and to drink with them. ⁵And it was so, when the days of their feasting were gone about, that Job sent and sanctified them, and rose up early in the morning, and offered burnt offerings according to the number of them all: for Job said, It may be that my sons have sinned, and renounced God in their hearts. Thus did Job continually.

6. Now there was a day when the sons of God came to present themselves before the LORD, and Satan came also among them. ⁷And the LORD said unto Satan, Whence comest thou? Then Satan answered the LORD, and said, From going to and fro in the earth, and from walking up and down in it. ⁸And the LORD said unto Satan, Hast thou considered my servant Job? for there is none like him in the earth, a perfect and an upright man, one that feareth God, and escheweth evil. ⁹Then Satan answered the LORD, and said, Doth Job fear God for nought? ¹⁰Hast not thou made an hedge about him, and about his house, and about all that he hath, on every side? thou hast blessed the work of his hands, and his substance is increased in the land. ¹¹But put forth thine hand now, and touch all that he hath, and he will renounce thee to thy face. ¹²And the LORD said unto Satan, Behold, all that he hath is in thy power; only upon himself put not forth thine hand. So Satan went forth from the presence of the LORD.

13. And it fell on a day when his sons and his daughters were eating and drinking wine in their eldest brother's house, ¹⁴that there came a messenger unto Job, and said, The oxen were plowing, and the asses feeding beside them: ¹⁵and the Sabeans fell *upon them*, and took them away; yea, they have slain the servants with the edge of the sword; and I only am escaped alone to tell thee. ¹⁶While he was yet speaking, there came also another, and said, The fire of God is fallen from heaven, and hath burned up the sheep, and the servants, and consumed them; and I only am escaped alone to tell thee. ¹⁷While he was yet speaking, there came also another, and said, The Chaldeans made three bands, and fell upon the camels, and have taken them away, yea, and slain the servants with the edge of the sword; and I only am escaped alone to tell thee. ¹⁸While he was yet speaking, there came also another, and said, Thy sons and thy daughters were eating and drinking wine in their eldest brother's house: ¹⁹and, behold, there came a great wind from the

wilderness, and smote the four corners of the house, and it fell upon the young men, and they are dead; and I only am escaped alone to tell thee. 20. Then Job arose, and rent his mantle, and shaved his head, and fell down upon the ground, and worshipped; ²¹and he said, Naked came I out of my mother's womb, and naked shall I return thither: the LORD gave, and the LORD hath taken away; blessed be the name of the LORD. ²²In all this Job sinned not, nor charged God with foolishness.

2. Again there was a day when the sons of God came to present themselves before the LORD, and Satan came also among them to present himself before the LORD. ²And the LORD said unto Satan, From whence comest thou? And Satan answered the LORD, and said, From going to and fro in the earth, and from walking up and down in it. ³And the LORD said unto Satan, Hast thou considered my servant Job? for there is none like him in the earth, a perfect and an upright man, one that feareth God, and escheweth evil: and he still holdeth fast his integrity, although thou movedst me against him, to destroy him without cause. ⁴And Satan answered the LORD, and said, Skin for skin, yea, all that a man hath will he give for his life. ⁵But put forth thine hand now, and touch his bone and his flesh, and he will renounce thee to thy face. ⁶And the LORD said unto Satan, Behold, he is in thine hand; only spare his life. ⁷So Satan went forth from the presence of the LORD, and smote Job with sore boils from the sole of his foot unto his crown. ⁸And he took him a potsherd to scrape himself withal; and he sat among the ashes. ⁹Then said his wife unto him, Dost thou still hold fast thine integrity? renounce God, and die. ¹⁰But he said unto her, Thou speakest as one of the foolish women speaketh. What? shall we receive good at the hand of God, and shall we not receive evil? In all this did not Job sin with his lips.

IN HEAVEN

HOWEVER familiar the opening scene of Job may be, there seem to be few who take it seriously. Most Christian depictions of Satan are entirely incompatible with what we are here told. We see Satan coming into the presence of God, and though it is not expressly stated, it is a fair inference that it was his duty so to do. What particular role he plays in the sovereign purposes of God is not made clear, though he goes up and down the world seeking whom he may accuse. But the vital point is that he is a servant of God, albeit an unwilling one. When in rabbinic tradition the personal name Sammael is given him with the office of angel of death, it is, of course, pure fancy, but the underlying principle is true.

The attitude of the liberal scholar tends to be that here we have a relatively primitive and outmoded conception of the Accuser (the meaning of Satan, which is a title, not a proper name). The more conservative scholar is apt to think that he need take only New Testament passages into consideration.

We must first of all remember that we cannot dismiss this picture as merely the expression of an old popular legend. Zech. 3: 1f and I Chron. 21: 1, the other two passages in the Old Testament where Satan is mentioned by name, express an identical outlook, as do Judges 9: 23, I Sam. 16: 14, 18: 10, 19: 9, I Kings 22: 19–23.

We must further bear in mind that the New Testament writers were familiar with the teaching of the Old and based themselves upon it. Even where they carried it further, they were affirming its truth. If then from the New Testament we have inferred views about the role and power of Satan which are in contradiction to the picture in *Job*, it means that by ignoring the Old Testament we have misunderstood the New.

It is not unfair to say that the vast majority of Christians either fly in the face of revelation and experience and deny the existence of Satan, or attribute to him such wide-reaching power and authority as to become virtual dualists in their religion. The teaching of Scripture is clear that nothing exists without God's will and permission. All power and authority are derived from Him. Whatever the position and power of Satan, he is God's creation, his power is derived from God, and willingly or unwillingly he is working out God's purposes. This is clearly seen in his conversation with God about Job.

It is usual to explain Job's sufferings by the malignity of Satan, but this is obviously false. Satan cannot even mention Job, for he has no accusation against him, until God invites him to do so (1: 8, 2: 3). Equally he has no power over Job or his possessions until God gives it him. So it is clear that, while God uses Satan's malignity, the origin of Job's sufferings goes back to God Himself, and no explanation of God's action is ever offered.

The fact that Satan is a fallen angel and in rebellion against God does not give to him any power at all except such as God chooses to give him. He is not sovereign in a rival kingdom, but a rebel to whom God gives as much rope as will glorify His own name.

Satan's fundamentally subservient role in the whole story is born out by his non-mention in the epilogue. Having carried out his task in stripping Job of wealth and health and in rousing Job's fellow-townsmen against him, he can be dismissed as of no further interest in the development of the story.

ON EARTH

The ease and speed with which all Job's wealth and happiness vanished once Satan was allowed to touch them should be to us not merely a reminder that the angel of the Lord encamps around those who fear Him, and delivers them, but also that it is God who rules in the affairs of men, and that He mercifully restrains the power of evil. We should be so concerned with the power of God, that the power entrusted to Satan will seem very small in comparison.

The pious Christian might have seen the hand of Satan in his loss and have prayed that he might be restrained. Probably more wisely, Job recognized the sovereignty of God. We are told that he did not charge God "with foolishness" (1: 22), but this is hardly an adequate translation, while "with wrong" (R.S.V.) is too strong. The Hebrew means "insipidity" or "unseemliness" (Koehler). It means that he did not consider that God had acted out of character; the I.C.C. is correct with "unworthiness."

There can be no certainty as to the nature of the disease with which Job was smitten. It may have been elephantiasis, a form of leprosy, or one of various oriental diseases proposed by doctors familiar with the Near East, or even smallpox, as recently suggested by Dr. Rendle Short.* It was not so much the pain of the disease that prostrated Job; it is referred to comparatively little in the speeches, and Stevenson, pp. 34ff, shows that in fact it may not be mentioned at all in them. It was that it had made him unclean, an outcast who found his resting place on the rubbish-mound outside the town gate. Though it is not stated in as many words, it is clear that Job's choice of the dung-hill (*the ashes*, 2: 8) outside the gate is not an expression of his despair, but it had been forced upon him because he had been thrust out by his fellow-townsmen.

Wetzstein writes in Delitzsch's *The Book of Job* about the dung-hills of the Hauran villages, now called *mezbele*:

"The dung . . . is carried in baskets in a dry state to that place outside the village, and there generally it is burnt once a month. . . . If a place has been inhabited for centuries, the *mezbele* attains a height far greater than that of the place itself. The rains of winter reduce the layers of ashes to a compact

---

* *The Bible and Modern Medicine*, p. 53f.

mass, and gradually convert the *mezbele* into a solid hill of earth. . . . There lies the outcast who, smitten by loathsome disease, is no longer admitted to the dwellings of men. . . . There lie the dogs of the village, gnawing perhaps some fallen carcase, such as is often thrown there."

For Job's contemporaries, as for the inhabitants of the Near East in general and for Israel in particular for many centuries to come, a man's prosperity or adversity, his health or sickness, were regarded as the verdict of heaven on his conduct. Job himself believed this, and this belief lies in one form or another behind all the arguments of his friends. The sting of this spiritual pain, of the belief that he was cast off by God, hurt far more than any physical suffering. But there was more to it than this. To be shut out of the fellowship of one's community was much worse. So great was the feeling of "corporate personality" that it was not till the spiritual victory of Jeremiah that men could realize that a man might be in fellowship with God even if he were cut off from his community. This explains the advice of Job's wife (2: 9). For her Job is as good as dead already, for he is not only ill, but cut off from God. For him to curse God and so bring swift and merciful relief in God's blasting death-stroke could not worsen his relationship to God. We can see the inner reality of Job's faith in that he does not allow his outward circumstances to overwhelm the inner witness of the Spirit within him. Though he cannot understand the reasons for his sufferings, he does not believe that God has cast him out. It should be noted that *in all this did not Job sin with his lips* does not imply in Hebrew, as it might well be construed in English, that Job sinned in his unspoken thoughts.

11. Now when Job's three friends heard of all this evil that was come upon him, they came every one from his own place; Eliphaz the Temanite, and Bildad the Shuhite, and Zophar the Naamathite: and they made an appointment together to come to bemoan him and to comfort him. 12And when they lifted up their eyes afar off, and knew him not, they lifted up their voice, and wept; and they rent every one his mantle, and sprinkled dust upon their heads toward heaven. 13So they sat down with him upon the ground seven days and seven nights, and none spake a word unto him: for they saw that his grief was very great.

We should not minimize the friendship of the three who came a long distance to comfort him. Although men of wealth and worth, they were not ashamed to associate with the outcast on the rubbish-mound. But fundamentally they had accepted without question the verdict of the men of his own town. The seven days and nights they sat with him (2: 13) are the period of mourning for the dead (cf. Gen. 50: 10, I Sam. 31: 13). In the name of friendship they tried to hide their convictions about Job, until he drove them to speak openly, but all their efforts at comfort were vitiated by their fundamental presupposition. Nothing ties us more readily than inherited superstitions.

CHAPTER IV

MY GOD! WHY?

AFTER this opened Job his mouth,
and cursed his day. ²And Job
answered and said:
³Let the day perish wherein I was
born,
and the night which said,
There is a man child conceived.
⁴Let that day be darkness;
let not God inquire after it from
above,
neither let the light shine upon
it.
⁵Let darkness and the shadow of
death claim it for their own;
let a cloud dwell upon it;
let all that maketh black the day
terrify it.
⁶As for that night, let thick darkness seize upon it:
let it not rejoice among the days of
the year;
let it not come into the number of
the months.
⁷Lo, let that night be barren;
let no joyful voice come therein.
⁸Let them curse it that curse the
day,
who are skilful to rouse up leviathan.
⁹Let the stars of the twilight thereof
be dark:
let it look for light, but have none;
neither let it behold the eyelids of
the morning:
¹⁰because it shut not up the doors of
my *mother's* womb,
nor hid trouble from mine eyes.
¹¹Why died I not from the womb?
why did I not give up the ghost
when I came out of the belly?
¹²Why did the knees receive me?
or why the breasts, that I should
suck?
¹³For now should I have lien down
and been quiet;

I should have slept; then had I
been at rest:
¹⁴with kings and counsellors of the
earth, which built up waste places
for themselves;
¹⁵or with princes that had gold,
who filled their houses with silver:
¹⁶or as an hidden untimely birth
I had not been;
as infants which never saw light.
¹⁷There the wicked cease from
troubling;
and there the weary be at rest.
¹⁸There the prisoners are at ease
together;
they hear not the voice of the task-
master.
¹⁹The small and great are there;
and the servant is free from his
master.
²⁰Wherefore is light given to him
that is in misery,
and life unto the bitter in soul;
²¹which long for death, but it
cometh not;
and dig for it more than for hid
treasures;
²²which rejoice exceedingly,
and are glad, when they can find
the grave?
²³*Why is light given* to man whose
way is hid,
and whom God hath hedged
in?
²⁴For my sighing cometh like my
meat,
and my roarings are poured out
like water.
²⁵For the thing which I fear cometh
upon me,
and that which I am afraid of
cometh unto me.
²⁶I am not at ease, neither am I
quiet, neither have I rest;
but trouble cometh.

29

As his friends sat there day after day, full of sympathy but unable to comfort—for what words of comfort can one speak to the sinner?—Job realized that it was not only the wicked of his own town and the fickle mob that had turned their backs on him, but also the wisest and best among his own friends. It may well be that Eliphaz, Bildad and Zophar were rising to leave, their period of mourning ended, when Job broke out into one of the most moving passages of the Bible.

As literature Job 3 is magnificent; so much so that it sweeps us along by its very vehemence and keeps our minds from asking what it all means.

He cursed the day of his birth (v. 1, R.S.V.). It is, alas, no rare experience to meet the man who has enjoyed health, riches and honour, who in middle life has lost all three and who longs for death. But it is most rare for such a one to say, at least with any conviction, unless indeed his conscience is already making him feel the flames of Hell, "I wish I had never been born." He has lived, and for most of the time living was good; even the final suffering cannot rob the earlier years of their sweetness. But it is precisely this that Job is saying with such vehemence. It is true the chapter ends (vv. 20–26) with the wish that he were dead, but this is subsidiary to the main thought.

There is only one strictly comparable passage in the Bible, viz. Jer. 20: 7–18). Not only is there an obvious literary resemblance between Jer. 20: 14–18 and Job 3: 3–10, however it is to be explained, but I believe a striking spiritual similarity between the two men can be demonstrated as well.

As a young man Jeremiah had followed the call of God to be a prophet. He could have reasonably expected recognition and honour, at least from the better elements among his people, and the joy of fellowship with God in his own heart. He found himself rejected by all and had apparently lost his relationship with God. I believe that in a very much simpler way this was true of Job as well. It is to be noticed that in this tremendous outburst Job does not refer to his material loss and physical affliction at all, unless it is by implication. It is only our knowledge of the circumstances that tempts us so to understand v. 24:

For my sighing comes as my bread,
    and my groanings are poured out like water (R.S.V.).

There is some element of doubt in vv. 25f. as to the best translation, but there can be little doubt that the translators of the
A.V. were misled by preconceived theory. The R.S.V., which
is substantially the same as the R.V., seems to give the meaning:

> For the thing that I fear comes upon me,
>   and what I dread befalls me.
> I am not at ease, nor am I quiet;
>   I have no rest; but trouble comes.

This is surely looking to something quite other than his physical
afflictions.

Let us take a closer look at Job himself. Throughout the book
he is presented, as are his friends, as a member of the highly
respected class of the Wise. He was obviously brought up in the
strict orthodoxy of the time, for which it was beyond dispute that
prosperity was the result and reward of godfearing goodness, and
disaster and suffering of wrongdoing. He is portrayed to us as
tam (1: 1, 8, 2: 3). The meaning of the word is "completeness"
rather than "perfection." All sides of his life and character were
harmoniously developed. The R.S.V. and Moffatt in rendering
"blameless," are probably as near as we can get to the thought of
the Hebrew. The whole orthodoxy of the time proclaimed that
this man should prosper, and in fact for many years he did. Then
disaster, absolute and horrible, swept over him. Since Job never
claims sinlessness, he might have welcomed some normal trouble
as the acceptable chastisement of God. But with the afflictions
that are his there is only one logical course for him to follow. He
must agree with the unanimous voice of the world and of his
friends and accept that he is the chief of sinners.

Here is Job's problem. If his theology is correct, he is the
chief of sinners, but he *knows* he is not. But if he listens to the
testimony of his own heart, then his theology, on which he has
built up his whole life, must be wrong. The fact that his con-
cepts of God and man are rudimentary compared to the highly
developed ones of Christian dogmatics does not mean that we are
not entitled to use the word theology, when speaking of him.
This thought is more agonizing even than the thought that he
may be the chief of sinners. So he finds that the firm moorings
of his life have vanished; that the ship of his life is adrift on the
dark ocean, without chart, without light, being carried he knows
not where.

He turns to his friends for sympathy, advice and comfort, but dogmatic orthodoxy has ever been without heart or understanding. It cannot conceive of religion as a vitally free fellowship with God, but insists on confining it to the Procrustean bed of man's limited understanding of the omnipotence and all-wisdom and love of God. But though they have no understanding for the plight of their friend, it is the three who really help Job back to peace, for they so increase his anguish that they drive him back to God. It is noticeable that in virtually all of Job's answers to his friends, while he first reacts to what has just been said, he then turns from his friends to God. Much that he says in his anguish is false and exaggerated, and some of it is virtually blasphemous, but what matters is that he turns to God.

CHAPTER V

THE DEBATE BEGINS

Eliphaz the Temanite (Chs. 4, 5)

THEN answered Eliphaz the
Temanite, and said,
²If one assay to commune with
thee, wilt thou be grieved?
but who can withold himself from
speaking?
³Behold, thou hast instructed many,
and thou hast strengthened the
weak hands.
⁴Thy words have upholden him
that was falling,
and thou hast confirmed the bow-
ing knees.
⁵But now it is come unto thee, and
thou faintest;
it toucheth thee, and thou art
troubled.
⁶Is not thy fear *of God* thy confidence,
and thy hope the integrity of thy
ways?
⁷Remember, I pray thee, who *ever*
perished, being innocent?
or where were the upright cut off?
⁸According as I have seen, they
that plow iniquity,
and sow mischief, reap the same.
⁹By the breath of God they perish,
and by the blast of his anger are
they consumed.
¹⁰The roaring of the lion, and the
voice of the fierce lion,
and the teeth of the young lions,
are broken.
¹¹The old lion perisheth for lack of
prey,
and the whelps of the lioness are
scattered abroad.
¹²Now a thing was secretly brought
to me,
and mine ear received a whisper
thereof.

¹³In thoughts from the visions of
the night,
when deep sleep falleth on men,
¹⁴fear came upon me, and trembling,
which made all my bones to shake.
¹⁵Then a breath passed over my
face;
the hair of my flesh stood up.
¹⁶It stood still, but I could not discern the appearance thereof;
a form was before mine eyes:
and I heard a still voice,
¹⁷Shall mortal man be just before
God?
shall a man be pure before his
Maker?
¹⁸Behold, he putteth no trust in his
servants;
and his angels he chargeth with
folly:
¹⁹how much more them that dwell
in houses of clay,
whose foundation is in the dust,
which are crushed like the moth!
²⁰Betwixt morning and evening they
are destroyed:
they perish for ever without any
regarding it.
²¹Is not their tent-cord plucked up
within them?
they die, and that without wisdom.

5. Call now; is there any that will
answer thee?
and to which of the holy ones wilt
thou turn?
²For vexation killeth the foolish
man,
and jealousy slayeth the silly one.
³I have seen the foolish taking root:
but suddenly I cursed his habitation.

C   33

⁴His children are far from safety,
and they are crushed in the gate,
neither is there any to deliver
them.
⁵Whose harvest the hungry eateth
up,
and taketh it even out of the
thorns,
and the snare gapeth for their
substance.
⁶For affliction cometh not forth of
the dust,
neither doth trouble spring out of
the ground;
⁷but man is born unto trouble,
as the sparks fly upward.
⁸But as for me, I would seek unto
God,
and unto God would I commit my
cause:
⁹which doeth great things and unsearchable;
marvellous things without number:
¹⁰who giveth rain upon the earth,
and sendeth waters upon the fields:
¹¹so that he setteth up on high those
that be low;
and those which mourn are exalted
to safety.
¹²He frustrateth the devices of the
crafty,
so that their hands can perform
nothing of worth.
¹³He taketh the wise in their own
craftiness:
and the counsel of the froward is
carried headlong.
¹⁴They meet with darkness in the
daytime,
and grope at noonday as in the
night.
¹⁵But he saveth from the sword of
their mouth,
even the needy from the hand of
the mighty.

¹⁶So the poor hath hope,
and iniquity stoppeth her mouth.
¹⁷Behold, happy is the man whom
God correcteth:
therefore despise not thou the
chastening of the Almighty.
¹⁸For he maketh sore, and bindeth
up;
he woundeth, and his hands make
whole.
¹⁹He shall deliver thee in six
troubles;
yea, in seven there shall no evil
touch thee.
²⁰In famine he shall redeem thee
from death;
and in war from the power of the
sword.
²¹Thou shalt be hid from the scourge
of the tongue;
neither shalt thou be afraid of
destruction when it cometh.
²²At destruction and dearth thou
shalt laugh;
neither shalt thou be afraid of the
beasts of the earth.
²³For thou shalt be in league with
the stones of the field;
and the beasts of the field shall be
at peace with thee.
²⁴And thou shalt know that thy
tent is in peace;
and thou shalt visit thy fold, and
shalt miss nothing.
²⁵Thou shalt know also that thy seed
shall be great,
and thine offspring as the grass of
the earth.
²⁶Thou shalt come to thy grave in a
full age,
like as a shock of corn cometh in in
its season.
²⁷Lo this, we have searched it, so it is;
hear it, and know thou it for thy
good.

O F Job's three friends Eliphaz is by far the most attractive. He is an obvious gentleman, sympathetic and courteous. While he will not compromise with his convictions, he does his best not to obtrude them too crudely until Job virtually forces him to. Then, for such is the character of an Eliphaz, he goes much farther than the others (ch. 22). However anachronistic it may be, I always see him, not in the robes of an eastern gentleman, but in frock coat, striped trousers and top hat, the revered vicar's warden or senior deacon of a wealthy and fashionable church.

Orthodoxy is in itself a very precious thing. It becomes hard, cruel and narrow when it becomes the expression of something other than a continuous living fellowship with the God of truth.

For Eliphaz his religious life revolved around a revelation that God had given him in a dream (4: 12–21):

A spirit glided past my face;
   the hair of my face stood up.
It stood still,
   but I could not discern its appearance.
A form was before my eyes;
   there was silence, then I heard a voice:
"Can mortal man be righteous before God?
Can a man be pure before his Maker?" (R.S.V.)

His dream left Eliphaz with a profound realization of the sinfulness of man, and it coloured his whole outlook on life from then on. But, as is so often the case with religious experiences, it became something complete in itself, something by which men could be measured and judged. There is absolutely nothing in all that Eliphaz says that suggests that it ever brought him to see that he was the chief of sinners, or that it drew him nearer God.

A religion without personal experience to which testimony can be borne is a poor thing, but there is a very real danger that where there is experience it may be equated with religion. When this happens, the victim of this delusion comes to think that there is little more to be reached, and that his experience is an infallible yard-stick by which he may measure the religion of others. We see this attitude all around us today; there are even denominations that make certain experiences the test of conversion or spirituality.

Eliphaz has much that is beautiful and true to say:

Who ever perished, being innocent?
   or where were the upright cut off?
According as I have seen, they that plough iniquity,
   and sow trouble, reap the same. . . .
But man is born unto trouble,
   as the sparks fly upward. . . .
Behold, happy is the man whom God reproveth:
   therefore despise not thou the chastening of the Almighty. . . .

He shall deliver thee in six troubles;
yea, in seven there shall no evil touch thee.

But behind all this truth and solicitude Job feels himself being poured into the mould of Eliphaz' experience. He may be too kind to pass judgment on his friend, but his whole bearing proclaims what the judgment would be, if it were spoken.

We have much to learn from Eliphaz. A gospel without experience will seldom warm the hearts of men, but an experience preached as the gospel will repel all but those cut in our pattern, while an experience that becomes the yard-stick of truth will turn itself into falsehood.

Job's Reply to Eliphaz (Ch. 6)

THEN Job answered and said,
2Oh that my vexation were but weighed,
and my calamity laid in the balances together!
3For now it would be heavier than the sand of the seas:
therefore have my words been rash.
4For the arrows of the Almighty are within me,
the poison whereof my spirit drinketh up:
the terrors of God do set themselves in array against me.
5Doth the wild ass bray when he hath grass?
or loweth the ox over his fodder?
6Can that which hath no savour be eaten without salt?
or is there any taste in the white of an egg?
7My soul refuseth to touch *them*;
they are as loathsome meat to me.
8Oh that I might have my request;
and that God would grant the thing that I long for!
9Even that it would please God to crush me;
that he would let loose his hand, and cut me off!
10Then should I yet have comfort;
yea, I would exult in pain that spareth not:
for I have not denied the words of the Holy One.

11What is my strength, that I should wait?
and what is mine end, that I should be patient?
12Is my strength the strength of stones?
or is my flesh of brass?
13Is it not that I have no help in me,
and that effectual working is driven quite from me?
14To him that is ready to faint kindness *should be shewed* from his friend;
even to him that forsaketh the fear of the Almighty.
15My brethren have dealt deceitfully as a brook,
as the channel of brooks that pass away;
16which are black by reason of the ice, *and* wherein the snow hideth itself:
17what time they wax warm, they vanish:
when it is hot, they are consumed out of their place.
18The caravans *that travel* by the way of them turn aside;
they go up into the waste, and perish.
19The caravans of Tema looked,
the companies of Sheba waited for them.
20They were ashamed because they had hoped;

they came thither, and were confounded.
²¹For now ye are nothing;
ye see a terror, and are afraid.
²²Did I say, Give unto me?
or, Offer a present for me of your
substance?
²³or, Deliver me from the adversary's hand?
or, Redeem me from the hand of
the oppressors?
²⁴Teach me, and I will hold my peace:
and cause me to understand wherein I have erred.
²⁵How forcible are words of uprightness!
but what doth your arguing
reprove?

²⁶Do ye imagine to reprove words?
seeing that the speeches of one that
is desperate are as wind.
²⁷Yea, ye would cast *lots* upon the
fatherless,
and make merchandise of your
friend.
²⁸Now therefore be pleased to look
upon me;
for surely I shall not lie to your
face.
²⁹Return, I pray you, let there be no
injustice;
yea, return again, my cause is
righteous.
³⁰Is there injustice on my tongue?
cannot my taste discern mis-
chievous things?

ONE word spoken by Eliphaz had pricked Job—*ka'as* (5: 2,
6: 2). *Ka'as*, which appears with far too wide a range of
renderings in the A.V., is our natural reaction of vexation,
impatience, grief and even anger, when faced with injustice and
offence. Only a fool will show it when rightly rebuked (Prov.
12: 15f), and only a fool will react this way when chastened by
God. (5: 2). The R.V., R.S.V. and I.C.C. render "vexation,"
while Knox prefers "impatience," but entirely misses the point
in Job's answer by using "provocation" in 6: 2; Moffatt's
"passion" is misleading. Eliphaz was in fact very unfair, for
Job had shown exemplary behaviour when calamity had fallen
on him (1: 20f.; 2: 10).

Faced with this determination on the part of his friends not to
take him as he is, but as a vindication of their principles, Job
reacts with his first vigorous rebuke. He pleads that calamity
as great as his may reasonably be allowed an outlet. In our
estimate of Job we must never forget his frank avowal that his
words have been rash (6: 3, R.V.) or wild (Moffatt). They have
been torn from him by anguish and are not the calm reflection of
theological reasoning.

We have an interesting confirmation in 6: 6, that Job's
sufferings were primarily spiritual. He compares them to taste-
less unsalted food and to the *slime of the purslane* (R.S.V., I.C.C.).
This would be a strange comparison if he were thinking of violent
pain that left him without a moment's ease, but we can see the
force of it, if he is thinking of mental suffering that makes him

shudder whenever he allows the thoughts to invade his mind, as
he shudders when faced with such food.   Sooner than live with
them he would die (6: 8f); the sense becomes clear when we realize
that the *pain that spareth not* (6: 10, R.V.) is the last pain of death.
Many have found difficulty in *For I have not denied the words
of the Holy One* (6: 10).   It is argued with justice that Job consistently speaks of Sheol, the abode of the dead, as a place where
all the dead are equal (3: 13–18), etc., hence it would make no
difference to him after death whether he had kept the words of
God or not.   But Job is typical of so many truly godly men.
He had been able to accept the popular view of rewards and
punishments without much thought, but when it was challenged
by experience he was prepared to abandon orthodoxy to feel after
God.   Similarly, while he shared in the then orthodox view of
Sheol, in the moment of crisis his knowledge of God told him that
there must be something beyond orthodoxy, and that at the last
God could not be indifferent to the life lived by man.   This is his
first step that is to lead him to that ray of light that for a moment
pierced beyond the grave (19: 25ff.).

The gist of Eliphaz' advice was that Job should submit himself
to God and wait trustfully: Job's scornful answer is that he will
be dead long before his friend's hope can be fulfilled (6: 11–14).
We are reminded of James' angry sarcasm in his Epistle (2: 15f.).
The three friends are then compared to one of the wadies of Trans-
jordan "bringing down great floods of dark and troubled waters
in spring," when they are least needed; but in the hour of need
in the summer heat it is dry.   All Job had asked of his friends
was understanding and sympathy, not money (6: 22) or valiant
deeds (6: 23).   Ironically enough, but entirely consistently with
human nature, he would probably have received the latter had
he asked for them.   True sympathy and understanding are
always costlier than charity.

THE MISERY OF LIFE (CH. 7)

Is there not a time of service to
man upon earth?
and are not his days like the days
of an hireling?
²As a servant that earnestly desireth the shadow,
and as an hireling that looketh for
his wages:

³so am I made to possess months of
vanity,
and wearisome nights are appointed to me.
⁴When I lie down, I say,
When shall I arise? but the night
is long;
and I am full of tossings to and

fro unto the dawning of the day.

⁵My flesh is clothed with worms and clods of dust;
my skin closeth up and breaketh out afresh.

⁶My days are swifter than a weaver's shuttle,
and are spent without hope.

⁷Oh remember that my life is wind:
mine eye shall no more see good.

⁸The eye of him that seeth me shall behold me no more:
thine eyes shall be upon me, but I shall not be.

⁹As the cloud is consumed and vanisheth away,
so he that goeth down to Sheol shall come up no more.

¹⁰He shall return no more to his house,
neither shall his place know him any more.

¹¹Therefore I will not refrain my mouth;
I will speak in the anguish of my spirit;
I will complain in the bitterness of my soul.

¹²Am I a sea, or a sea-monster,
that thou settest a watch over me?

¹³When I say, My bed shall comfort me,

my couch shall ease my complaint;

¹⁴then thou scarest me with dreams,
and terrifiest me through visions:

¹⁵so that my soul chooseth strangling,
and death rather than *these* my bones.

¹⁶I loathe *my life*; I would not live alway:
let me alone; for my days are vanity.

¹⁷What is man, that thou shouldest magnify him,
and that thou shouldest set thine heart upon him,

¹⁸and that thou shouldest visit him every morning,
and try him every moment?

¹⁹How long wilt thou not look away from me,
nor let me alone till I swallow down my spittle?

²⁰If I have sinned, what do I unto thee, O thou watcher of men?
why hast thou set me as a mark for thee,
so that I am a burden to myself?

²¹And why dost thou not pardon my transgression,
and take away mine iniquity?
For now shall I lie down in the dust;
and thou shalt seek me diligently,
but I shall not be.

IT was probably the look of troubled or cold incomprehension on his friends' faces that made Job look away from them to God. *Remember* (7: 7) is in the singular, and is addressed to God, not to Job's friends; there is no need to doubt that this holds good for the whole chapter.

As we trace our way through the book we find that Job's sufferings bring him not only to a truer knowledge of God but also to a more living knowledge of his fellow men. As he turned from the puzzled incomprehension of his friends, he suddenly realized with a start that it was not only he whom they failed to understand, and that his lot was far from being unique. It was all very well for Eliphaz to fold his hands over his plump belly and say sententiously, *Man is born unto trouble, as the sparks fly upward*. It was true enough, but it meant all too little to him.

But when Job breaks out, *Is there not hard labour for man upon earth? and are not his days like the days of an hireling?* (7: 1), for a moment we are introduced to the solidarity of suffering. But it is only in Christ that the solidarity of suffering can become really constructive. For Job it only increased his burden, for now he saw it as only an aggravation of misery ample in itself.

Remarkably enough, Job's increased vision of suffering did not shake his trust in God. With a touching naïvety he says, *Thine eyes shall be upon me, but I shall not be* (7: 8). It is quite understandable that the rabbis should be upset by a man like Choni the Circle-drawer,* of whom Simeon ben Shetach said that he behaved petulantly before God as a son behaves before his father. But both in public and in private prayer there is a strange lack of willingness among many Christians to be completely frank with their heavenly Father. This is one of the greatest lessons we can learn from Jeremiah and Job. They never hesitated to open their hearts to God, even though men might call their words blasphemy. Here Job suggests that God has in some strange aberration forgotten His normal behaviour and that when the mood is over He will look for Job to be kind to him again, but it will then be too late, for he will be among the dead.

There follow some of Job's bitterest words (7: 11–21), which he must have regretted with all his heart, after God had revealed Himself to him. Job has been led to reject the orthodoxy in which he had been reared and which Eliphaz has been repeating to him, but so far he cannot grasp that God may be doing something entirely alien to man's beliefs about Him. It is a weakness of ours to assume, when in real or pretended humility we acknowledge that we do not understand God's working in any particular circumstance, that we are dealing merely with an uncommon variant of the normal. Man hates to say that he does not understand what God's intentions may be. That is why our comfort and advice so often miss the mark with those who suffer. So Job assumes that his sufferings must have some relation to his sins. He tells God, using popular mythological language, that after all he has never been, like the powers of Chaos, a rebel against Him, nor has his sin, whatever it may have been, injured the majesty

---

* Among the stories told of him is that in a time of great drought he drew a circle in the dust and told God that he was not going to step outside it until God gave rain. When a downpour followed, he told God that they did not want a flood but suitable rain for the fields. In this too he was heard.

of the Almighty. Once again, in v. 21, he takes up the thought of v. 8, and says that when God changes His mind it will be too late, for he will be gone.

BILDAD THE SHUHITE (CH. 8)

THEN answered Bildad the Shuhite, and said,

²How long wilt thou speak these things?
and *how long* shall the words of thy mouth be *like* a mighty wind?

³Doth God pervert judgement?
or doth the Almighty pervert justice?

⁴If thy children sinned against him, and he delivered them into the hand of their transgression:

⁵if thou wouldest seek diligently unto God,
and make thy supplication to the Almighty;

⁶if thou wert pure and upright;
surely now he would awake for thee,
and make the habitation of thy righteousness prosperous.

⁷And though thy beginning was small,
yet thy latter end should greatly increase.

⁸For inquire, I pray thee, of the former age,
and apply thyself to that which their fathers have searched out:

⁹(for we are but of yesterday, and know nothing,
because our days upon earth are a shadow:)

¹⁰shall not they teach thee, and tell thee,
and utter words out of their heart?

¹¹Can the papyrus grow up without mire?
can the reed-grass grow without water?

¹²Whilst it is yet in its greenness, *and* not cut down,
it withereth before any *other* herb.

¹³So are the paths of all that forget God;
and the hope of the godless man shall perish:

¹⁴whose confidence shall be cut off, and whose trust is a spider's web.

¹⁵He shall lean upon his house, but it shall not stand:
he shall hold fast thereby, but it shall not endure.

¹⁶He is green before the sun, and his shoots go forth over his garden.

¹⁷His roots are wrapped about the heap,
he beholdeth the place of stones.

¹⁸If he be destroyed from his place, then it shall deny him, *saying*, I have not seen thee.

¹⁹Behold, this is the joy of his way, and out of the earth shall others spring.

²⁰Behold, God will not cast away a perfect man,
neither will he uphold the evildoers.

²¹He will yet fill thy mouth with laughter,
and thy lips with shouting.

²²They that hate thee shall be clothed with shame;
and the tent of the wicked shall be no more.

BILDAD is in many ways the most dogmatic of the three friends. He is not as downright brutal as Zophar, but he is more pitiless. He is the only one to refer to the fate of Job's children:

If your children have sinned against Him,
He has delivered them into the power of their transgression (8: 4),

where the "if" is of course a polite "because." Left to himself
he would probably have been a humble and likeable man, but he
had constituted himself a champion of the orthodoxy of the past.
If he had lived at a later period, he would willingly have burnt
Job's body in the hope of saving his soul.

His position is made clear in 8: 8ff.:

For inquire, I pray you, of bygone ages,
    and consider what the fathers have found;
for we are but of yesterday, and know nothing,
    for our days on earth are a shadow.
Will they not teach you, and tell you,
    and utter words out of their understanding? (R.S.V.)

Bildad is a pillar of the Church and a champion of orthodoxy.
We can ill do without him and he has a rare gift of recognizing the
first insidious inroads of false doctrine. Just because he has no
axe to grind, because he is the faithful depository of the wisdom
and experience of the past, he is often a valued and revered
teacher. But for all that he is apt to be the Church's worst friend
in the hour of change and of crisis. Above all, when men are sore
tried and distressed, and the landmarks of life are hidden, it is
seldom to Bildad that they turn.

I cannot think of Bildad without contrasting him with John
Robinson at Delfshaven in 1620, as he speaks to the members of
his church leaving for the new world:

"I charge you before God and His blessed angels, that you
follow me no farther than you have seen me follow the Lord
Jesus Christ. If God reveals anything to you by any other
instruments of His, be as ready to receive it as you were to
receive any truth by my ministry, for I am verily persuaded the
Lord hath more truth yet to break forth out of His holy word.
For my part, I cannot sufficiently bewail the condition of those
reformed churches which are come to a period in religion, and
will go, at present, no farther than the instruments of their
reformation. The Lutherans cannot be drawn to go beyond
what Luther saw; whatever part of His will our God has
revealed to Calvin, they will rather die than embrace it; and
the Calvanists, you see, stick fast where they were left by that
great man of God, who yet saw not all things. . . ."

Entirely consistently with his inherited theology, Bildad can only see life as it conforms to the pattern set for it.   Characteristically, where Eliphaz had spoken of the foolish and had seen all men with their share of suffering, Bildad speaks of the perfect— *tam*, cf. 1: 1 and p. 31—and the evil-doers (8: 20), and the wicked (8: 22).   These last, the *resha'im*, are to recur repeatedly from this time on.   We would do well to notice that it is not sinners in general who are intended.   A study of the passages where they are mentioned will show that they are rich and mighty men, such as Job was before his calamity, who, however, flaunt their wickedness in the sight of God and man.   The problem of the wicked in Job is not concerned with the secret sinner or the small man ground down in life, but with those for whom there is no excuse in their sinning.

It would seem at first reading that Bildad was merely shocked at the wildness of Job's words and that he was really convinced of his essential innocence (8: 20f.).   When, however, he says,

> Will the papyrus rise up proudly without mire?
> Will the reed-grass grow without water? (8: 11, I.C.C.)

he seems to be suggesting that there is no smoke without fire. His real feelings are suddenly revealed at the very end, when he says, *And the tent of the wicked shall be no more* (8: 22b); we cannot doubt that he is thinking of Job's loss of all things.   Though he is holding open the door of repentance to Job, he leaves no doubt that he considers him one of the wicked on whom the well-merited judgments of God have fallen.

Job's Reply to Bildad (Ch. 9: 1–24)

Then Job answered and said,
  [2]Of a truth I know that it is so:
but how can man be just with
  God?
[3]If one should desire to contend
  with him,
he could not answer him one of a
  thousand.
[4]*He is* wise in heart, and mighty in
  strength:
who hath hardened himself against
  him, and prospered?
[5]Which removeth the mountains,
  and they know it not,
when he overturneth them in his
  anger.

[6]Which shaketh the earth out of
  her place,
and the pillars thereof tremble.
[7]Which commandeth the sun, and
  it riseth not;
and sealeth up the stars.
[8]Which alone stretcheth out the
  heavens,
and treadeth upon the waves of the
  sea.
[9]Which maketh the Bear, Orion,
  and the Pleiades,
and the chambers of the south.
[10]Which doeth great things past
  finding out;

yea, marvellous things without number.

11Lo, he goeth by me, and I see him not:
he passeth on also, but I perceive him not.

12Behold, he seizeth *the prey*, who can hinder him?
who will say unto him, What doest thou?

13God will not withdraw his anger;
the helpers of Rahab did stoop under him.

14How much less shall I answer him, and choose out my words *to reason* with him?

15Whom, though I were righteous, yet would I not answer;
I would make supplication to mine adversary.

16If I had called, and he had answered me;
yet would I not believe that he hearkened unto my voice.

17For he breaketh me with a tempest,

and multiplieth my wounds without cause.

18He will not suffer me to take my breath,
but filleth me with bitterness.

19If *we speak* of the strength of the mighty, lo, *he is there*!
and if of judgement, who will appoint me a time?

20Though I be righteous, mine own mouth shall condemn me:
though I be perfect, he shall prove me perverse.

21I am perfect; I regard not myself;
I despise my life.

22It is all one; therefore I say,
He destroyeth the perfect and the wicked.

23If the scourge slay suddenly,
he will mock at the calamity of the innocent.

24The earth is given into the hand of the wicked:
he covereth the faces of the judges thereof;
if *it be* not *he*, who then is it?

JOB knew Bildad from of old, and doubtless he anticipated all he had to say as soon as he opened his mouth. So there are no wild reproaches in his answer.

I pointed out in ch. II that we are dealing with wisdom literature, with men striving by their wisdom to discover the ways of God. The everlasting power and divinity of God are revealed to us in God's creation (Rom. 1: 20), but the moral character of God is only truly recognizable in the sphere of redemptive revelation— and Job and his friends were not even within the covenant of Sinai, still less the new covenant. We should never forget that man's conscience is very far from being an infallible guide to God's moral demands on men. Its purpose is rather to insist that God does make such demands.

Job accepts Bildad's insistence on the justice of God (8: 3), but sets it in a new setting. When Eliphaz said, *Can mortal man be righteous before God?* (4: 17), he was thinking of the sinfulness of man. Job takes up the thought (9: 2), but makes it mean that man is not in the position to establish his right before God, for God always has the *power* to prove him wrong. There are in the law of Moses certain apparently arbitrary commandments which have been the despair of commentators. The only reasonable interpretation to be placed on them is that they are a revelation of a sovereign power that has the right to impose arbitrary commands. Certainly in the experience of the saints there are happenings which cannot be explained by finite man, though doubtless we shall understand them in eternity. Job tells his friends that—apart from revelation—there is no evidence of God's moral government in the affairs of this world.

He then strangely anticipates God's own revelation to him, and on the basis of God's all-might challenges the possibility of knowing God's ways;

Lo, He goeth by me, and I see Him not:
He passeth on also, but I perceive Him not (9: 11)

is a challenge to the whole concept that God's ways are essentially understandable. What to his friends is even worse, he flatly denies their whole interpretation of life:

The earth is given into the hand of the wicked:
He covereth the faces of the judges thereof;
if it be not He, who then is it? (9: 24).

We shall see that the major part of their later discussion revolves around this statement by Job.

But how is it that men living in the same land, brought up together, can come to such diametrically opposed views of society? Life around us is so rich and manifold that if we are to understand any of its manifestations we must learn to choose those phenomena that are significant and virtually to ignore the rest. That is what the scientist is doing all the time. But few of us are trained scientists or observers. We normally see what we want to see, and overlook or minimize that which does not suit our theories. The teaching of the Wise was based on carefully selected facts. When Job had to suffer, his eyes were opened to the suffering around him; when he felt the smart of injustice, he saw for the first time clearly the prevalence of injustice around him. We know that Job's friends were wrong; we must not jump to the conclusion that Job was right. They and he alike are giving us partial views of reality, but, for all that, Job tends to see more of the essentials than they do. Each in his own way, Job's friends see the world through the spectacles of their respective theories. Job has no theory; he is an explorer of new realms.

Even though his observation is distorted by passion and suffering, it still remains nearer the truth than the picture which has to conform to preconceived ideas.

We do well to remember this. God's estimate of man and his life is not the sinner's, and the world is seldom willing to welcome the proclamation of human sin. It is seldom, however, that the man caught up in a system sees the world as it is revealed to us in the Scriptures. The more authoritarian the system, the more distorted its view of the world and of man. The captives of the system, especially our Bildads, sincerely reverence God's revelation and wish to know His will and do it. For all that they insist that revelation and will must conform to their understanding and tradition, and so they fail to grasp either.

THE POTTER AND THE CLAY (CHS. 9: 25–10: 22)

23Now my days are swifter than a runner:
they flee away, they see no good.
26They are passed away as the ships of reed:
as the eagle that swoopeth on the prey.
27If I say, I will forget my complaint, I will put off my *sad* countenance, and be of good cheer:
28I am afraid of all my sorrows, I know that thou wilt not hold me innocent.
29I shall be condemned; why then do I labour in vain?
30If I wash myself with snow, and cleanse my hands with lye;
31yet wilt thou plunge me in the ditch, and mine own clothes shall abhor me.
32For he is not a man, as I am, that I should answer him, that we should come together in judgement.
33There is no umpire betwixt us, that might lay his hand upon us both.
34Let him take his rod away from me, and let not his terror make me afraid:

35then would I speak, and not fear him; for I am not so in myself.

10. My soul is weary of my life; I will give free course to my complaint; I will speak in the bitterness of my soul.
2I will say unto God, Do not condemn me; shew me wherefore thou contendest with me.
3Is it good unto thee that thou shouldest oppress, that thou shouldest despise the work of thine hands, and shine upon the counsel of the wicked?
4Hast thou eyes of flesh, or seest thou as man seeth?
5Are thy days as the days of man, or thy years as man's days,
6that thou inquirest after mine iniquity, and searchest after my sin,
7although thou knowest that I am not wicked; and there is none that can deliver out of thine hand?
8Thine hands have framed me and fashioned me together round about; yet thou dost destroy me.

⁹Remember, I beseech thee, that thou hast fashioned me as clay; and wilt thou bring me into dust again?

¹⁰Hast thou not poured me out as milk, and curdled me like cheese?

¹¹Thou hast clothed me with skin and flesh, and knit me together with bones and sinews.

¹²Thou hast granted me life and favour, and thy visitation hath preserved my spirit.

¹³Yet these things thou didst hide in thine heart; I know that this *is* with thee:

¹⁴if I sin, then thou markest me, and thou wilt not acquit me from mine iniquity.

¹⁵If I be wicked, woe unto me; and if I be righteous, yet shall I not lift up my head; being filled with ignominy and looking upon mine affliction.

¹⁶And if *my head* exalt itself, thou huntest me as a lion: and again thou shewest thyself marvellous upon me.

¹⁷Thou renewest thy witnesses against me, and increasest thine indignation upon me, changes and warfare are with me.

¹⁸Wherefore then hast thou brought me forth out of the womb? I had given up the ghost, and no eye had seen me.

¹⁹I should have been as though I had not been; I should have been carried from the womb to the grave.

²⁰Are not my days few? cease then, and let me alone, that I may take comfort a little,

²¹Before I go whence I shall not return, to the land of darkness and of the shadow of death;

²²A land of thick darkness, as darkness *itself*; of the shadow of death, without any order, and where the light is as darkness.

JOB had not proclaimed the power of God to his friends as a mere abstract principle. The time was soon to come when the knowledge of the all-might of God, not as grasped by his own intellect but as revealed by God Himself, would bring peace to the wounded soul of Job. But that was not yet. At the moment he was overwhelmed; shut in on every side by a power he neither knew nor understood, he refused to abandon his belief that it was merciful and loving, and yet he could see no signs of mercy and love. He longed to come before His judgment seat and reason his case before Him, and yet he knew he could never prove his case. So when he had thrown down his challenge to Bildad (9: 24), he turned to speak to God. In this section Job no longer speaks about God, but to Him; indeed we may question how far his friends were even intended to hear him.

There are few more affecting passages in Scripture. Here is a broken man, who has lost all. Racked with pain and troubled in heart, he yet refuses to listen either to his fellow townsfolk or to his friends. He knows himself a sinner, yet he cannot believe that God has cast him off. He longs for a daysman, an umpire,

between him and His God, but not to Job was there given a vision
of the Mediator who was to come. So he turns in trembling hope
to his Creator, but all he can ask for is a few days of brightness
before he goes *to the land of darkness and of the shadow of death*
(10: 21).

Zophar the Naamathite (Ch. 11)

THEN answered Zophar the Naamathite, and said,
²Should not the multitude of words
be answered?
and should a man full of talk be
justified?
³Should thy boastings make men
hold their peace?
and when thou mockest, shall no
man make thee ashamed?
⁴For thou sayest, My doctrine is
pure,
and I am clean in thine eyes.
⁵But Oh that God would speak,
and open his lips against thee;
⁶and that he would shew thee the
secrets of wisdom,
that it is manifold in effectual
working!
Know therefore that God remitteth unto thee of thine iniquity.
⁷Canst thou find out the deep things
of God?
canst thou find out the Almighty
unto perfection?
⁸It is high as heaven; what canst
thou do?
deeper than Sheol; what canst
thou know?
⁹The measure thereof is longer than
the earth,
and broader than the sea.
¹⁰If he pass through, and shut
up,
and call unto judgement, then who
can hinder him?
¹¹For he knoweth vain men:

he seeth iniquity also, even though
he consider it not.
¹²But an empty man will get understanding,
when a wild ass's colt is born a
man.
¹³If thou set thine heart aright,
and stretch out thine hands toward him;
¹⁴if iniquity be in thine hand, put it
far away,
and let not unrighteousness dwell
in thy tents;
¹⁵surely then shalt thou lift up thy
face without spot;
yea, thou shalt be stedfast, and
shalt not fear:
¹⁶for thou shalt forget thy misery;
thou shalt remember it as waters
that are passed away:
¹⁷and *thy* life shall be clearer than
the noonday;
though there be darkness, it shall
be as the morning.
¹⁸And thou shalt be secure, because
there is hope;
yea, thou shalt search *about thee*,
and shalt take thy rest in safety.
¹⁹Also thou shalt lie down, and none
shall make thee afraid;
yea, many shall make suit unto
thee.
²⁰But the eyes of the wicked shall
fail,
and they shall have no way to flee,
and their hope shall be the giving
up of the ghost.

WHETHER or not Job intended his words to God to be heard
and taken in by his friends, they drove Zophar to fury,
and he could hardly refrain from interrupting. As soon
as Job had finished, he brushed all to one side as just "words."
He is the typical man of common sense, for whom life holds few

problems, and who is suspicious of him who finds them, and still more of him who discusses them.

It is not that he is not a God-fearing man, but simply that the mysteries of God do not concern him, for they are too high:

> Canst thou find out the deep things of God?
> Canst thou find out the Almighty unto perfection?
> It is high as heaven; what canst thou do?
> deeper than Sheol; what canst thou know? (11: 7f).

For him Job's "Why?" is Job's greatest sin, the supreme proof that he had not even begun to walk in the paths of Wisdom:

> An empty man will get understanding,
> when a wild ass's colt is born a man (11: 12).

All Job has to do is to set his heart aright and pray and put away iniquity (11: 13f.) and all will be perfectly all right.

All of us are familiar with Zophar. He is the man who is perpetually demanding the simple Gospel, by which he does not mean the greatest mystery of God's love expressed so that a child can understand it, but God's love stripped of all mystery. He looks on every doubt as being in itself sin, and every difficulty as the sign of an evil heart of unbelief. The neurotic and the mentally ill receive short shrift at his hands, and he generally has some authority, not over profound, appeal to whom settles every controversy. He is uneasy the moment intellectual discussion begins, and he finds the late Professor Joad's famous opening gambit, "It all depends on what you mean by . . .", a sign of intellectual dishonesty. To suggest to him that a verse of Scripture may bear a different sense than does its plain meaning in the Authorised Version is the cloven hoof of modernism, while to appeal to the Greek and the Hebrew is mere sophistry.

The Church needs its Zophars. They are a salutary check upon us when we grow too abstract, too clever, too intellectual, when we feed the flock on wind and speculation. Their shrewd common sense will often show a committee the obvious, and they often strip the veil of make-believe from man's heart. But for all that, God have mercy on Job when he falls into Zophar's hands!

Eliphaz is too gentlemanly to be over-harsh with Job, until Job rouses him to theological fury. Bildad is too humble to want to sit as judge on Job himself; he would rather that the voices of the past should judge. But Zophar does not hesitate: *Know therefore*

D

that God remitteth unto thee of thine iniquity (11: 6), i.e. compared with what Job's sin deserves his calamities are very forgiveness itself.

JOB'S REPLY TO ZOPHAR (CHS. 12: 1–13: 19)

THEN Job answered and said,
   ²No doubt but ye are the people,
and wisdom shall die with you.
³But I have understanding as well as you;
I am not inferior to you:
yea, who knoweth not such things as these?
⁴I am as one that is a laughing-stock to his neighbour,
a *man* that called upon God, and he answered him:
the just, the perfect man is a laughing-stock.
⁵In the thought of him that is at ease there is contempt for misfortune;
it is ready for them whose foot slippeth.
⁶The tents of robbers prosper,
and they that provoke God are secure;
that bring *their* God in their hand.
⁷But ask now the beasts, and they shall teach thee;
and the fowls of the air, and they shall tell thee:
⁸or speak to the earth, and it shall teach thee;
and the fishes of the sea shall declare unto thee.
⁹Who knoweth not by all these,
that the hand of the LORD hath wrought this?
¹⁰In whose hand is the soul of every living thing,
and the breath of all mankind.
¹¹Doth not the ear try words,
even as the palate tasteth its meat?
¹²With aged men is wisdom,
and in length of days understanding.
¹³With him is wisdom and might;
he hath counsel and understanding.

¹⁴Behold, he breaketh down, and it cannot be built again;
he shutteth up a man, and there can be no opening.
¹⁵Behold, he withholdeth the waters,
and they dry up;
again, he sendeth them out, and they overturn the earth.
¹⁶With him is strength and sound wisdom;
the deceived and the deceiver are his.
¹⁷He leadeth counsellors away spoiled,
and judges maketh he fools.
¹⁸He looseth the bond of kings,
and bindeth their loins with a girdle.
¹⁹He leadeth priests away spoiled,
and overthroweth the mighty.
²⁰He removeth the speech of the trusty,
and taketh away the understanding of the elders.
²¹He poureth contempt upon princes,
and looseth the belt of the strong.
²²He discovereth deep things out of darkness,
and bringeth out to light the shadow of death.
²³He increaseth the nations, and destroyeth them:
he spreadeth the nations abroad, and bringeth them in.
²⁴He taketh away the heart of the chiefs of the people of the earth,
and causeth them to wander in a wilderness where there is no way.
²⁵They grope in the dark without light,
and he maketh them to stagger like a drunken man.

13. Lo mine eye hath seen all *this*,
mine ear hath heard and understood it.

²What ye know, *the same* do I know also:
I am not inferior unto you.
³Surely I would speak to the Almighty,
and I desire to reason with God.
⁴But ye are forgers of lies,
ye are all physicians of no value.
⁵Oh that ye would altogether hold your peace!
and it should be your wisdom.
⁶Hear now my reasoning,
and hearken to the pleadings of my lips.
⁷Will ye speak unrighteously for God,
and talk deceitfully for him?
⁸Will ye respect his person?
will ye contend for God?
⁹Is it good that he should search you out?
or as one deceiveth a man, will ye deceive him?
¹⁰He will surely reprove you,
if ye do secretly respect persons.
¹¹Shall not his excellency make you afraid,

and his dread fall upon you?
¹²Your memorable sayings *are* proverbs of ashes,
your defences *are* defences of clay.
¹³Hold your peace, let me alone, that I may speak,
and let come on me what will.
¹⁴Wherefore should I take my flesh in my teeth,
and put my life in mine hand?
¹⁵Though he slay me, yet will I wait for him:
nevertheless I will maintain my ways before him.
¹⁶This also shall be my salvation;
that a godless man shall not come before him.
¹⁷Hear diligently my speech,
and let my declaration be in your ears.
¹⁸Behold now, I have ordered my cause;
I know that I shall be justified.
¹⁹Who is he that will contend with me?
for now shall I hold my peace and give up the ghost.

ACED with Bildad's appeal to the past, Job must have felt helpless trying to answer a man who would not think for himself. Faced with Zophar's brutal common sense that made all revolve around his own understanding, he felt hopeless, and for a moment he broke out in bitter sarcasm: *No doubt but ye are the people* [i.e. all the wisdom of the world is found in you, and so] *wisdom shall die with you* (12: 2). Sarcasm has its place in the Christian's armoury, for sometimes it is the only way to deflate the proud complacency of the self-satisfied. But Job's barb is too weak to puncture the hide of these champions of orthodoxy. He would have needed a harpoon at the least: as it is he only pricks and angers them.

A new thought now begins to emerge. The fact that his friends failed to understand him, were unable to comfort him, and even condemned him for imagined sin, were painful but bearable. But now has come Zophar's bitter jibe about the ass's colt (11: 12, R.V. mg.). Job sees his position among the Wise denied, attributed doubtless to his skill in learning the right answers by rote; his asking of awkward questions is considered merely a sign of stupidity. Job's friends have been caught in the trap that always lies hidden for the defenders of orthodoxy, however the term be defined, *viz.* the belief that failure to agree with the dominant majority must be due to intellectual, moral or spiritual faults. With their falling into this trap the discussion tends to move from Job and his personal sufferings (though these remain in the forefront) to the wider problem of whether the experience and speculation of the Wise enable them to dogmatize on the working out of God's will among men.

Had the wisdom shown by his friends been something exceptional, it might have been bearable, but Zophar's shallow agnosticism is infuriating. What of it if a righteous man like Job becomes a laughing-stock? God used to answer his prayers—no matter! Men used to find nothing to criticize in him (*perfect*, 12: 4)—what of it? On the other hand, violent men, who know no other god than their weapons (*that bring their god in their hand*, 12: 6, R.V. mg.), prosper—oh, well, God knows the answer to such anomalies! The all-might of God is something so obvious that even birds and beasts and fishes know that God stands behind all that happens (12: 7)—though modern man has often fallen below the level of the brute creation in this! For Zophar to suggest that Job did not know this is a gratuitous insult (13: 1f.).

There is little agreement as to how we should interpret 12: 11–25 R.V. mg., Moffatt, Peake, I.C.C., Strahan all find a contrast between vv. 12 and 13; in other words Job is rejecting the basis of Bildad's confidence (8: 8) and inferentially of his friends as well, and proclaiming that in God alone is wisdom. To me it seems far more likely that Job is continuing his sarcasm. After re-affirming the maxim they had constantly heard, when they had first sat at the feet of the Wise:

> With aged men is wisdom,
>   and in length of days understanding (12: 12),

he heaps aforism on aforism:

> All God's doing; his are the wisdom and the power; to him belong prudence in act and discernment. The ruins he makes, none can rebuild, his imprisonment none can escape; withholds he the rain, all is dried up; sends he rain, it floods all the ground. Yes, he is strong, he is wise; reads the knave's heart as easily as the fool's. He can thwart the counsellor, bemuse the judge, exchange the king's baldrick for the rope of a prisoner, lead the priest away ungowned, dispossess the noble, bewitch the lips

that never erred, rob the elder of his prudence, bring princes into contempt, unman the strong. Things deep hidden in darkness he reveals, kindles the light where death's shadow lay, brings growth or ruin to a people, and what he has ruined restores. The hearts of chieftains he bewilders, leading them by false paths to vain ends, till all light fails, and they grope about in darkness, wander aimless like a drunkard after wine (12: 13–25, Knox).

Yes, of course all this is true, and Job can say it as well or better than his friends, but the unspoken question remains: How much nearer are we to understanding God's ways and works?

But Job cannot believe that God is merely the Unknowable. He wants to speak to the Almighty and argue things out with Him (13: 3). His original cry of "Why?" had been an invitation to his friends to help him in this quest. But he had found them mere windbags, standing up for God with sophistries and empty maxims. The wish to defend God from the attacks and complaints of men may be natural and laudable, but in the case of Job's friends, as so often, there was less concern for God's glory and more for a parade of their own wisdom. But even where the motives are correct it is apt to be love's labour lost. God can look after Himself, and we always run the grave risk of re-creating Him in our own image before we are ready "to justify His ways to men" (13: 4–12).

It had been agony for Job to lose his comfortable, ready-made views of God's providence, and he recognizes that it is taking his life in his hand (13: 14) to seek an interview with God and to argue things out with Him. To this many will say Amen; they will point to those who, unsatisfied with the old orthodoxies, have sought to know more and more fully and have made shipwreck of their faith. This is, alas, all too true, but where this is so, the motive of the search has often been at fault, and they have sought the answer by the wrong means. We must hesitate in judgment, however, for often enough the heresies of yesterday are the orthodoxies of today, and where we have thought of shipwreck, they have been sailing unknown seas and gathering great wealth.

Job is emboldened in his undertaking, for he knows that a godless man would not and could not so come before God (13: 16). So strongly does his faith blaze forth that he assures his genuinely horror-struck friends, *I know I shall be justified* (13: 18), and tells them that if any can bring a justified charge against him, *then would I hold my peace and give up the ghost* (13: 19). Job is so confident that, if God will but lift his afflictions for the moment and veil His glory, he is content to be either plaintiff or defendant.

JOB PLEADS HIS CAUSE (CHS. 13: 20–14: 22)

20 ONLY do not two things unto me,
then will I not hide myself from thy face:
21withdraw thine hand far from me; and let not thy terror make me afraid.
22Then call thou, and I will answer; or let me speak, and answer thou me.
23How many are mine iniquities and sins?
make me to know my transgression and my sin.
24Wherefore hidest thou thy face, and holdest me for thine enemy?
25Wilt thou harass a driven leaf? and wilt thou pursue the dry stubble?
26For thou writest bitter things against me,
and makest me to inherit the iniquities of my youth:
27thou puttest my feet also in the stocks, and markest all my paths; thou drawest thee a line about the soles of my feet:
28though I am like a rotten thing that consumeth,
like a garment that is moth-eaten.

14. Man that is born of a woman is of few days, and full of trouble.
2He cometh forth like a flower, and is cut down:
he fleeth also as a shadow, and continueth not.
3And dost thou open thine eyes upon such an one,
and bringest me into judgement with thee?
4Who can bring a clean thing out of an unclean?
not one.
5Seeing his days are determined,
the number of his months is with thee,
and thou hast appointed his bounds that he cannot pass;
6look away from him, that he may rest,
till he shall accomplish, as an hireling, his day.
7For there is hope of a tree, if it be cut down, that it will sprout again,
and that the tender branch thereof will not cease.
8Though the root thereof wax old in the earth,
and the stock thereof die in the ground;
9yet through the scent of water it will bud,
and put forth boughs like a plant.
10But man dieth, and wasteth away: yea, man giveth up the ghost, and where is he?
11*As* the waters fail from the sea, and the river decayeth and drieth up;
12so man lieth down and riseth not: till the heavens be no more, they shall not awake,
nor be roused out of their sleep.
13Oh that thou wouldest hide me in Sheol,
that thou wouldest keep me secret, until thy wrath be past,
that thou wouldest appoint me a set time, and remember me!
14If a man die, shall he live *again*? all the days of my warfare would I wait,
till my release should come.
15Thou shouldest call, and I would answer thee:
thou wouldest have a desire to the work of thine hands.
16But now thou numberest my steps:

dost thou not watch over my sin?

¹⁷My transgression is sealed up in a bag,
and thou fastenest up mine iniquity.

¹⁸And surely the mountain falling cometh to nought,
and the rock is removed out of its place;

¹⁹the waters wear the stones;
the overflowings thereof wash away the dust of the earth:

and thou destroyest the hope of man.

²⁰Thou prevailest for ever against him, and he passeth;
thou changest his countenance, and sendest him away.

²¹His sons come to honour, and he knoweth it not;
and they are brought low, but he perceiveth it not of them.

²²But his flesh upon him hath pain, and his soul within him mourneth.

AFTER his bold declaration of confidence as to the outcome of his hearing before God (13: 20ff.) Job begins by demanding to know what God has against him: *How many are my iniquities and my sins? Make me know my transgression and my sin* (13: 23). This is not in itself a declaration of guilt. All along Job's thesis is that, while he is a sinner, he is not so in a measure that would justify his sufferings. He offers God the unexpressed alternative of revealing sins that would justify his sufferings or of motivating his sufferings on some other ground. Obviously it is the latter that he really expects.

Here we must imagine a dramatic pause. Job looks vainly to the brazen vault of heaven for an answer, while his friends huddle together in startled fear lest a thunderbolt or fire from heaven should silence the blasphemy. But neither hope nor fear is fulfilled.

Job continues by pleading that if there are no such sins to reveal he is too insignificant for God to make such an example of him (13: 24–28). By *the iniquities of my youth* we must not understand that Job had sown his wild oats as a young man. He is rather suggesting that the only conceivable reason for his suffering is as insignificant as the sufferer himself.

Since God will not answer Job's plea, Job turns and arraigns God. He affirms that not only is God's treatment of Job unworthy, but so is His treatment of men in general (14: 1–12). Job cries, *Oh that a clean thing could come out of an unclean! Not one can* (14: 4). Since all the severity of God can never transform man, God should *look away from* man in his frailty, for all too soon he will go to his "long home." Job is not here asking God to cease being from the judge of all the earth. Even when he later questions the morality of God's rule, he does so with fear in his

heart, lest by any means he might be correct. He is here concerned with the ordinary man, more sinned against than sinning,
more labouring than enjoying the fruits of his lands, more suffering
than rejoicing.

The ancient Israelites, or rather those among them from whom
sprang the writers of the Old Testament, so lived in consciousness
of Jehovah's presence and favour that they were normally able
to live in the passing moment, looking neither to the disappointed
hopes of yesterday nor to their fears for tomorrow. For them the
present, blessed by the presence of God, was essentially good, and
so the Old Testament tends to be an optimistic book. From time
to time, however, the writer detaches himself from the present
and looks on life as a whole. Then a pessimistic note, gilded it
is true with the sunshine of God, breaks through. Death stands
there in the shadows, bringing to naught all man's efforts and
achievements. Job sees the irony that while the cut-down or
dying tree may yet live (14: 7ff—a common phenomenon in
tropical and sub-tropical climates, cf. Is. 6: 13, 11: 1, R.V., and
better R.S.V.) no such hope awaits man.

Western civilization today is essentially optimistic. We can
so drug ourselves with luxuries, machine-made entertainment and
the "security" of the welfare state that neither the certainty of
death nor the threat of nuclear weapons brings us to look on life
as a whole. "Life is worth living" is the slogan of our age. Is it
mere coincidence that the suicide rate is highest in those lands
and among those social classes where it is easiest to refuse to see
life as it really is? It is interesting how there is a growing tendency, which reaches its climax in North America, to wrap death
in decent obscurity by the skill of the undertaker, the crematorium
and the park-cemetery. The modern man revolts against the old
hymn:

> Time, like an ever-rolling stream,
> Bears all its sons away;
> They fly forgotten, as a dream
> Dies at the opening day.

For all that there stands written over all life, even more clearly
than for Job, "It is appointed unto man once to die, and after
this the judgment."

SHEOL

We cannot think otherwise of God than as the origin of all wisdom and rational thought. For all that, there is in God's wisdom and logic an element too high for man's mind to grasp; He says, "My ways are higher than your ways, and My thoughts than your thoughts." Logically the view should be correct that when man dies he ceases to exist. Man is above all *nephesh*, which in suitable contexts our older translations consistently render "soul." This is most unfortunate, for neither in popular use nor in the normal understanding of dogmatic theology do the two words approximate in meaning.

Nephesh is the *totality* that results when body and spirit are united. The R.S.V. and Moffatt render Gen. 2: 7 far more satisfactorily by "and man became a living being"; Knox's "a living person" is perhaps even better. When the body returns to the dust and the spirit returns to Him who gave it, logically the *nephesh*, the personality of man, should vanish. In fact the Old Testament teaches that it continues a shadow existence in Sheol (New Testament, Hades). It is a shadow existence because there is no spirit to impel it to action, and no body through which it can act, but for all that the *nephesh* continues to vegetate unimpaired.

In 3: 11–26, Job had craved death, but subsequently we find the conflict between this longing and the desire for a little peace and sunshine before the inevitable end comes. In ch. 14 Job reacts doubly against death: not merely is there the longing for a few peaceful hours, but his natural fear of death and its finality has reasserted itself. Once more (cf. 7: 8, 21) the thought rises that God's anger with him must be some strange passing aberration. He fears, however, that he cannot hold out until it passes, and so he prays (14: 13) in agony that he may enjoy all the advantages of death without its finality. Then, startled, he realizes where his thoughts have led him: *If a man die, shall he live again?* The answer implied is clearly "No." We must, however, note clearly that Job is not thinking of resurrection in Christian terms, but of a continuance of life which death has interrupted. Even if we were to supply the answer "Yes," the end of this living again would again be death.

Though as yet it is a striking thought regretfully to be pushed away, were it possible for him to have a new span of life lived out under God's smile and favour, he would gladly bear *all the days of my service* (14: 14) in the agony of this life and in the waiting in Sheol. As it is, all he has to hope for is a period of unexplained suffering followed by a name forgotten among men, and the hopeless and purposeless existence of Sheol.

> Thou destroyest the hope of man.
> Thou prevailest for ever against him, and he passeth;
> Thou changest his countenance, and sendest him away.
> His sons come to honour, and he knoweth it not;
> And they are brought low, but he perceiveth it not.

So ends the first round of the debate. Job's three friends have revealed clearly how each, according to his own character and experience, has prejudged him whom he called friend by trying to accommodate his case to his own wonted measuring rod. Job has writhed under his friends' condemnation and lack of sympathy and understanding. The heavens have been silent to reproach and appeal alike. Broken Job collapses on the dung-hill as he accepts that death with all its finality is all that he can expect.

It does not end here, however, for orthodoxy has been outraged and is on the war-path looking for blood.

CHAPTER VI

THE SECOND ROUND

"I AM OFFENDED" (CH. 15)

THEN answered Eliphaz the Temanite, and said,
²Should a wise man make answer
with vain knowledge,
and fill his belly with the east
wind?
³Should he reason with unprofitable
talk,
or with speeches wherewith he can
do no good?
⁴Yea, thou doest away with fear,
and restrainest devotion before
God.
⁵For thine iniquity teacheth thy
mouth,
and thou choosest the tongue of
the crafty.
⁶Thine own mouth condemneth
thee, and not I;
yea, thine own lips testify against
thee.
⁷Art thou the first man that was
born?
or wast thou brought forth before
the hills?
⁸Hast thou heard the secret counsel
of God?
and dost thou restrain wisdom to
thyself?
⁹What knowest thou, that we know
not?
what understandest thou, which is
not in us?
¹⁰With us are both the grayheaded
and the very aged men,
much elder than thy father.
¹¹Are the consolations of God too
small for thee,
and the word *that dealeth* gently
with thee?
¹²Why doth thine heart carry thee
away?
and why do thine eyes wink?

¹³That thou turnest thy spirit
against God,
and lettest *such* words go out of
thy mouth.
¹⁴What is man, that he should be
clean?
and he which is born of a woman,
that he should be righteous?
¹⁵Behold, he putteth no trust in his
holy ones;
yea, the heavens are not clean in
his sight.
¹⁶How much less one that is abomin-
able and corrupt,
a man that drinketh iniquity like
water!
¹⁷I will shew thee, hear thou me;
and that which I have seen I will
declare:
¹⁸which wise men have told
from their fathers, and have not
hid it;
¹⁹unto whom alone the land was
given,
and no stranger passed among
them:
²⁰the wicked man travaileth with
pain all his days,
even the number of years that are
laid up for the oppressor.
²¹A sound of terrors is in his
ears;
in prosperity the spoiler shall come
upon him:
²²he believeth not that he shall
return out of darkness,
and he is waited for of the sword:
²³he wandereth abroad for bread,
saying, Where is it?
he knoweth that the day of darkness is ready at his hand:
²⁴distress and anguish make him
afraid;

they prevail against him, as a king ready to the battle:
²⁵because he hath stretched out his hand against God,
and behaveth himself proudly against the Almighty;
²⁶he runneth upon him with a *stiff* neck,
with the thick bosses of his bucklers:
²⁷because he hath covered his face with his fatness,
and made collops of fat on his flanks;
²⁸and he hath dwelt in desolate cities,
in houses which no man inhabited, which were ready to become heaps.
²⁹He shall not be rich, neither shall his substance continue,
neither shall their produce bend to the earth.

³⁰He shall not depart out of darkness;
the flame shall dry up his branches, and by the breath of his mouth shall he go away.
³¹Let him not trust in vanity, deceiving himself:
for vanity shall be his recompence.
³²It shall be accomplished before his time,
and his branch shall not be green.
³³He shall shake off his unripe grape as the vine,
and shall cast off his flower as the olive.
³⁴For the company of the godless shall be barren,
and fire shall consume the tents of bribery.
³⁵They conceive mischief, and bring forth iniquity,
and their belly prepareth deceit.

SILENCE lay for a while over the dung-hill until it was broken by Eliphaz' voice. There is a sharp edge to it now and a spot of red on his cheeks. He is trying hard to keep his temper, and as his words begin to roll out a little of the old graciousness returns. But it is clear that Eliphaz has been really shocked and offended.

"Are you one of the Wise, Job? What wise man would talk like you?" (vv. 2f). Urbanity and moderation, the carefully turned phrase and balanced aphorism, these have always been beloved in the schools of learning. When our Lord looked around Him with anger (Mark 3: 5) or called His opponents "ye serpents, ye offspring of vipers" (Matt. 23: 33), the Pharisees, like so many of their modern descendants, were doubtless shocked that one who was called Rabbi should so lower His dignity. They probably said, "After all He is only one of the *am ha-aretz* (common people) from Galilee." But there are times when the hard facts of life demand the sweeping away of sophistries which try to empty them of true meaning.

"Job, you speak like a godless man and you will encourage others to follow your example" (vv. 4ff.). Eliphaz always loves to make his own standards the pattern of behaviour, and he will always be found turning to the alleged perils of the "younger brother" as a good motive for condemning what he does not approve of. In my own experience I have generally found the "younger brother" strangely tough. He is all for a bit of experiment and is apt to think of Eliphaz as an old stick-in-the-mud, if not worse. It is unchristian living by the professedly Christian leader that makes him stumble.

"Job, you are suffering from swelled head, you want to know what only the superhuman could know" (vv. 7f.). The Christian will quite cheerfully discuss the mystery of the Trinity; he will dogmatize how man and God could co-exist in the person of the Messiah; he will peer down the vistas of time and draw up a timetable for the future. But when you take him by the back of the neck and rub his nose on some of the facts of life, he is promptly up in arms, and appeals to the inscrutable wisdom of God.

"Job, you are claiming to know more than *we*, than *I*, who am old enough to be your father"—this is the meaning of verse 10. Here is the rub. Eliphaz, who has based his whole theology on experience, feels that a challenge to his theology is a challenge to his experience, a challenge to his yard-stick, a challenge to his personal integrity, especially when it comes from a much younger man.

I once received a letter from a well-known Christian: How can you write like that to a man of my age and position? That he had wantonly slandered me obviously did not trouble his conscience. That he had no answer to my rebuttal of his charges against me left him unmoved. My sin was that I had ventured to reject his judgment.

So once again Eliphaz repeats the teaching of chs. 4 and 5. But now the shadows have been increased. The picture of the sinfulness of man (vv. 14ff.) is darker, and it is clear enough that Eliphaz would be ill-pleased, if you perversely saw *him* in the picture; it is Job he is thinking of. Then, with a glance at Bildad, he appeals to the things most surely believed, the undiluted traditions of the fathers (vv. 17ff.). Before our eyes is unrolled the tragic life and death of Mr. Badman (vv. 20–35); whose first name is, of course, Job, if only he will recognize himself.

It is easy to smile as we picture Eliphaz leaning forward in his eagerness, a little pompously and a little breathlessly reaching a triumphant conclusion in which he sees the wicked not merely going down to a premature grave, but leaving nothing but disaster behind him. But whether it was the pious young man asking me incredulously how there could be "pleasures of sin" (Heb. 11:25), or those who deny that there can be piety and a knowledge of God among the Roman Catholics (or any other denomination they dislike, for that matter), or who affirm that unless you have conformed to something external you cannot be a Christian, or who commiserate with Judaism as being nothing more than sterile legalism, this is always the voice of Eliphaz, who subordinates fact to theory.

JOB SOLILOQUIZES (CHS. 16, 17)

THEN Job answered and said,
²I have heard many such things:
miserable comforters are ye all.
³Shall vain words have an end? or what provoketh thee that thou answerest?
⁴I also could speak as ye do; if your soul were in my soul's stead,
I could join words together against you,
and shake mine head at you.
⁵*But* I would strengthen you with my mouth,
and the solace of my lips should assuage *your grief.*
⁶Though I speak, my grief is not assuaged:
and though I forbear, what am I eased?
⁷But now he hath made me weary: thou hast made desolate all my company.
⁸And thou hast laid fast hold on me, *which* is a witness *against me:*
and my leanness riseth up against me, it testifieth to my face.
⁹He hath torn me in his wrath, and persecuted me;
he hath gnashed upon me with his teeth:
mine adversary sharpeneth his eyes upon me.
¹⁰They have gaped upon me with their mouth;
they have smitten me upon the cheek reproachfully:
they gather themselves together against me.
¹¹God delivereth me to the ungodly,

and casteth me into the hands of the wicked.
¹²I was at ease, and he brake me asunder;
yea, he hath taken me by the neck, and dashed me to pieces:
he hath also set me up for his mark.
¹³His archers compass me round about,
he cleaveth my reins asunder, and doth not spare;
he poureth out my gall upon the ground.
¹⁴He breaketh me with breach upon breach;
he runneth upon me like a giant.
¹⁵I have sewed sackcloth upon my skin,
and have laid my horn in the dust.
¹⁶My face is red with weeping, and on my eyelids is the shadow of death;
¹⁷although there is no violence in mine hands,
and my prayer is pure.
¹⁸O earth, cover not thou my blood, and let my cry have no *resting* place.
¹⁹Even now, behold, my witness is in heaven,
and he that voucheth for me is on high.
²⁰My friends scorn me:
but mine eye poureth out tears unto God;
²¹that he would maintain the right of a man with God,
and of a son of man with his neighbour!
²²For when a few years are come,

I shall go the way whence I shall not return.

17. My spirit is consumed, my days are extinct,
the grave is *ready* for me.
²Surely there are mockers with me,
and mine eye abideth in their provocation.
³Give now a pledge, be surety for me with thyself;
who is there that will strike hands with me?
⁴For thou hast hid their heart from understanding:
therefore shalt thou not exalt *them*.
⁵He that denounceth his friends for a prey,
even the eyes of his children shall fail.
⁶He hath made me also a byword of the people;
and I am become one in whose face they spit.
⁷Mine eye also is dim by reason of sorrow,
and all my members are as a shadow.
⁸Upright men shall be astonied at this,
and the innocent shall stir up himself against the godless.
⁹Yet shall the righteous hold on his way,
and he that hath clean hands shall wax stronger and stronger.
¹⁰But return ye, all of you, and come now:
and I shall not find a wise man among you.
¹¹My days are past, my purposes are broken off,
even the thoughts of my heart.
¹²They change the night into day:
the light, *say they*, is near unto the darkness.
¹³If I look for Sheol as mine house;
if I have spread my couch in the darkness;
¹⁴if I have said to corruption, Thou art my father;
to the worm, *Thou art* my mother, and my sister;
¹⁵where then is my hope?
and as for my hope, who shall see it?
¹⁶It shall go down to the bars of Sheol,
when once there is rest in the dust.

ONCE he had answered Eliphaz for the first time (ch. 6), Job had grown ever less interested in what his friends had to say, for they were only repeating the platitudes in which he had been brought up himself. Zophar woke a spark of sarcasm, but Eliphaz' indignation produces only a dignified rebuke. He reminds them that they are only repeating themselves (16: 2a), and that after all they had come to comfort him (16: 2b, cf. 2: 11). As Knox renders it, *Old tales and cold comfort; you are all alike.* After all, if they could not comfort, they were under no compulsion to say anything.

The futility of Eliphaz' pomposity did not stir Job as Zophar's jibes had done, and seated, as it were, between God and his friends he begins a soliloquy in which, while he may address one side or the other, he speaks mainly to himself.

Neither speaking nor silence has had much effect on his condition (16: 6). After all, there was not much purpose in blaming his friends, for it was God who had treated him as though he were

guilty (16: 7f.). If God had acted as though He were a wild animal (16: 9, 12a,b.), he could not blame men for acting similarly
(16: 10). He had been the mark for God's arrows (16: 12c, 13),
a fortress attacked by the strongest of warriors (16: 14). In spite
of all, his reply had been humility and prayer (16: 15ff). *I have
sewed sackcloth upon my skin* implies the permanence of his mourning. Among the Arabs one may under certain circumstances sew
oneself into a garment, so that it cannot be removed without cut-
ting the seams. Job is not referring to his friends in verse 11, but
to the great, evil men who have rejoiced at the downfall of a pillar
of righteousness.

Job had never doubted that sooner or later God would change
His attitude towards him (7: 8, 21, 14: 13ff.), though he had no
hope that friends or enemies would. So he calls on the earth
(16: 18) to keep on crying to God till He hears—for He, the just
one, is already his witness—and proclaims that he was in
spite of all right with God (16: 21). Perhaps nowhere more
strongly than in 17: 3, does Job suggest a contradiction in God
Himself: God is to become surety for Job that his cause will be
vindicated with God. Such language may shock us, but in fact
there can be few children of God who have not at one time or
another faced this very problem. There IS an apparent contradiction in God's acts, and it is only as our eyes are fixed on the
power and love of God that it disappears.

Since the vision of God's power is yet future, Job, left in his
perplexity, gives a pitying glance at his friends (17: 4) and maintains that he will *hold on his way* (17: 9)—verses 8f. surely refer
to Job himself—even though the hopes of physical recovery held
out to him by his friends are false (17: 12–16).

Not only is the translation of 17: 5 very doubtful, but however
we render it, it seems almost impossible to give a satisfactory
meaning to it in its setting. A reference to Moffatt *ad loc.* will
show to what straits he is driven.

The Fate of Mr. Badman (Ch. 18)

THEN answered Bildad the Shuhite, and said,

²How long will ye lay snares for
words?
consider, and afterwards we will
speak.

³Wherefore are we counted as
beasts,

and are become unclean in your
sight?

⁴Thou that tearest thyself in thine
anger,
shall the earth be forsaken for
thee?
or shall the rock be removed out of
its place?

⁵Yea, the light of the wicked shall be put out,
and the flame of his fire shall not shine.

⁶The light shall be dark in his tent, and his lamp above him shall be put out.

⁷The steps of his strength shall be straitened,
and his own counsel shall cast him down.

⁸For he is cast into a net by his own feet,
and he walketh upon the toils.

⁹A gin shall take *him* by the heel, a snare shall lay hold on him.

¹⁰A noose is hid for him in the ground,
and a trap for him in the way.

¹¹Terrors shall make him afraid on every side,
and shall chase him at his heels.

¹²His strength shall be hunger-bitten,
and calamity shall be ready for his halting.

¹³It shall devour the members of his body,
the firstborn of death shall devour his members.

¹⁴He shall be rooted out of his tent wherein he trusteth;
and he shall be brought to the king of terrors.

¹⁵There shall dwell in his tent that which is none of his:
brimstone shall be scattered upon his habitation.

¹⁶His roots shall be dried up beneath, and above shall his branch be cut off.

¹⁷His remembrance shall perish from the earth,
and he shall have no name in the street.

¹⁸He shall be driven from light into darkness,
and chased out of the world.

¹⁹He shall have neither son nor son's son among his people,
nor any remaining where he sojourned.

²⁰They that dwell in the west shall be astonied at his day,
as they that dwell in the east were affrighted.

²¹Surely such are the dwellings of the unrighteous,
and this is the place of him that knoweth not God.

BILDAD was in his own way as annoyed as Eliphaz; but because he stood for a cause and not some personal interest he could control his feelings better. He honestly could not understand the attitude of the man who rejected the wisdom of the past. It was clear that "there is nothing new under the sun," and obviously the wisdom of the great saints and theologians must have taken a case like Job's into consideration.

So he breaks out:

Ah, you wordmongers, you have never had enough! First grasp our meaning, and we might argue to some purpose; but no, to men like thee we are worthless as dumb beasts. See with what fury he tears his own bosom! (18: 2ff, Knox).

It is quite likely that the last remark is looking back to Job's words in 16: 9. Bildad believes that Job is just trying to keep his end up by wilfully misunderstanding his friends.

So he takes up the story of Mr. Badman again and turns it with a cold pitilessness against Job.   Eliphaz is to go farther (ch. 22), but loses his temper in doing so and makes a fool of himself, thus defeating his own ends.   Your traditionalist, however, is too conscious of the weight of the past behind him to allow his feelings to be involved.   If Eliphaz was sufficient of a gentleman to describe the fate of Mr. Badman in general, conventional terms (15: 20–35), perhaps Bildad was correct after all in suggesting that Job had not wanted to understand Eliphaz.   Well, he will not misunderstand Bildad, who leaves nothing to chance!

He begins, therefore, as did the story of Job's misfortunes, with the extinction of Mr. Badman's family (18: 5ff.).   Most commentaries understand the *light* and the *lamp* as referring to prosperity and happiness, but II Sam. 21: 17, I Kings 11: 36, 15: 4, II Kings 8: 19, Psalm 132: 17, all suggest most strongly that it is life and above all descendants that are intended.   Where there is life in an oriental dwelling there will be a light at night.   Psalm 127: 3ff., is a telling commentary on v. 7a.

In vv. 8–11 we have the unrecorded consequences of 1: 13–22, unrecorded because to an Oriental they were self-evident.   The wicked and evil had risen against him (cf. 16: 10f.), and even his own kin had disowned him (cf. 19: 13–19).   Then follows (vv. 11ff.) a reference to Job's physical sufferings, and Bildad finishes in cold satisfaction with a picture of his certain end (vv. 14–21). Amen! so shall be the fate of Job!

Eliphaz, after time for reflection, may see that he has been defending his own experience, Zophar may possibly realize that human common sense is inadequate to cope with the divine, and so they may in time come to terms with the world's Jobs, but not so Bildad.   The world must conform to his pattern, for it is divinely given; where such things are in fashion he will excommunicate, persecute and even burn the man he considers to be under the judgment of God, in the hope of saving his soul.

"I KNOW THAT MY VINDICATOR LIVETH" (CH. 19)

THEN Job answered and said,
²How long will ye vex my soul,
and break me in pieces with words?
³These ten time have ye reproached me:
ye are not ashamed that ye deal hardly with me.

⁴And be it indeed that I have erred,
mine error remaineth with myself.
⁵If indeed ye will magnify yourselves against me,
and plead against me my reproach:
⁶know now that God hath subverted me *in my cause*,

and hath compassed me with his net.

⁷Behold, I cry out, Violence! but I am not heard:
I cry for help, but there is no judgement.

⁸He hath fenced up my way that I cannot pass,
and hath set darkness in my paths.

⁹He hath stripped me of my glory, and taken the crown from my head.

¹⁰He hath broken me down on every side, and I am gone:
and mine hope hath he plucked up like a tree.

¹¹He hath also kindled his wrath against me,
and he counteth me unto him as *one of* his adversaries.

¹²His troops come on together, and cast up their way against me,
and encamp round about my tent.

¹³He hath put my brethren far from me,
and mine acquaintance are wholly estranged from me.

¹⁴My kinsfolk have failed,
and my familiar friends have forgotten me.

¹⁵They that dwell in mine house, and my maids, count me for a stranger:
I am an alien in their sight.

¹⁶I call unto my servant, and he giveth me no answer,
I intreat him with my mouth.

¹⁷My breath is strange to my wife, and I am loathsome to the children of my *mother's* womb.

¹⁸Even young children despise me; if I arise, they speak against me.

¹⁹All my inward friends abhor me:
and they whom I loved are turned against me.

²⁰My bone cleaveth to my skin and to my flesh,
and I am escaped with the skin of my teeth.

²¹Have pity upon me, have pity upon me, O ye my friends;
for the hand of God hath touched me.

²²Why do ye persecute me as God, and are not satisfied with my flesh?

²³Oh that my words were now written!
oh that they were inscribed in a book!

²⁴That with an iron pen and lead they were graven in the rock for ever!

²⁵But I know that my vindicator liveth,
and that he shall stand up at the last upon the earth:

²⁶and after my skin hath been thus destroyed,
yet without my flesh shall I see God:

²⁷whom I shall see on my side, and mine eyes shall behold, and not another.
My reins are consumed within me.

²⁸If ye say, How we will persecute him!
seeing that the root of the matter is found in me;

²⁹be ye afraid of the sword:
for wrath *bringeth* the punishments of the sword,
that ye may know there is a judgement.

JOB does not deign to answer Bildad's accusation. He tells his friends what he had already boldly said to God (7: 20a), that even if he had sinned his sin was no concern of theirs (19: 4).

Sin is a social offence, an offence against individuals, and an offence against God. Those who are called to rule and judgment must deal with sin in its first capacity. If we have been personally sinned against we have a duty to the sinner, at least if he is a member of the Church (Matt. 18: 15ff.). Otherwise we have no concern with the sins of others, only with the sinner. Our purpose should not be to try to persuade men to sin less, a process that may produce Pharisees, but not saints, but to turn the sinner to God. We must preach that men are sinners, but we dare not sit in judgment and assess the quantity and quality of their sins.

Job's friends had undoubtedly judged Job secretly on the basis of the scale of his sufferings even before he spoke. Once he had implicitly challenged their judgment, they were not concerned with showing that he was a sinner (Job knew that quite well), but that he was a great sinner. They were not concerned so much with turning him to God as with getting him to acquiesce in their judgment. When they spoke of the greatness of God, it was to bludgeon Job, not to draw him to God. Job's friends are with us today, as they have ever been in the Church. That is why the worldly man shrinks from the pious but not from saints. The open sinners in the time of Christ shrank from the Pharisees but flocked to our Lord.

The greatest wrong his friends did Job was resolutely to refuse to see that he was genuine in his efforts to come to terms with God. So now he reminded them once again that he really had a complaint against God (vv. 5–12). This had been aggravated by the behaviour of kith and kin (vv. 13f.); his slaves, male and female, had forgotten their duty (vv. 15f.); his wife had lost her affection for him (taking *My breath is strange to my wife* metaphorically, as does Stevenson), and his pleas to brothers and sisters remained unheard (v. 17); even the little children refused him the honour due to his age (v. 18). He turned to his friends for a little sympathy, a little understanding (v. 21), but we may suppose that he met nothing but the cold glance of bewilderment and anger.

It is hard enough for a Christian to be silent when he is calumniated, even though he knows that he can trust his Lord to care for his honour. For Job, to whom honour meant more than it does to us, the thought that God and man had joined together to drag his honour in the dust meant more than physical suffering or material loss. He declared that if only he could write his vindication on a scroll, or better still engrave it in stone, then surely a generation would come that would vindicate him (vv. 23f.)

But what would be the use of human vindication, when his controversy was with God? Suddenly the conviction we have noted before, the conviction of a strange duality in God, a God who is temporarily unjust, but who will yet remember His former mercy and love, flared up into white light.   The verses (25ff.) in which Job expressed his new insight have led to much controversy among translators and commentators, but the following seems a fair rendering of them:

> I know that my Vindicator lives
>   and will yet stand upon the earth;
> and after my skin has been thus destroyed,
>   then without my flesh shall I see God,
> whom I shall see on my side,
>   and my eyes shall see to be unestranged.
> My heart fails with longing within me.

Job had no hope of vindication in this life, but now he knew God *must* vindicate him.   But (and here is the leap of faith) a vindication in which he did not share would be a hollow mockery, so he knew that he would see this hour, bodiless though he might be; yes, he would see God unestranged!   He nearly swooned at the thought.

There is no need to justify the rendering "Vindicator."   It is given by R.V. mg., R.S.V., and is accepted explicitly or implicitly by almost all moderns.   Job calls God his *go'el*; the *go'el* was a man's near kinsman, whose duty was the avenging of wrong, e.g. as avenger of blood, or the redeeming of the man, when he had become a slave, or of his property.   When the term is used of God (either the substantive or the cognate verb), as it is particularly in the Psalms and Isa. 40–66, it obviously receives a much richer meaning.   In our context Job is thinking neither of healing nor of resurrection, as A.V. and R.V. tx. might suggest.   He is concerned with the clearing of his good name and hence "Vindicator" expresses the sense best—a similar rendering would suit Pr. 23: 11, and it is implicit in a number of passages where we must retain "redeemer."

A vindication that is not shared, we have already said, is a hollow thing and so Job is brought to the confidence of Ps. 139: 8, where David realizes that communion with God is possible in Sheol, and above all to that of Pss. 73: 23f., 17: 15, that death cannot break off a communion with God begun in this life.   In other words it is continued conscious communion with God after death rather than the resurrection of the body that Job is proclaiming.

Far more important than an exact definition of Job's hope of

There is little need to occupy ourselves with the details of
Zophar's picture of Mr. Badman. He adds little to Eliphaz'
picture in ch. 15. The chief new element is his insistence on the
brevity of Mr. Badman's enjoyment of the fruits of evil. Here
too we see a weakness of common sense. Eliphaz was, after all,
generalizing from an imperfect knowledge of God and of human
life, but at least he based himself on facts. Zophar, once he has
accepted the theories of the Wise, does not need facts; to him it
is obvious that if Mr. Badman is under the judgment of God,
judgment must fall suddenly and soon. Yes, obvious, but . . .!

One thing Zophar spares Job. He is too annoyed and too little
of a man of theory to work out a parallel between his picture of
Mr. Badman and the plight of his friend as did Bildad. He does,
however, prepare the way for Eliphaz (ch. 22). As a shrewd man
of common sense he must have been puzzled by the lack of concrete accusations they could bring against a man who must
obviously have been guilty of heinous offences, if they were to
judge by his sufferings. So he indirectly accuses him of the
commonest of all offences of the rich against the poor (20: 19),
i.e. land-grabbing and oppression.

MR. BADMAN'S PROSPERITY (CH. 21)

THEN Job answered and said,
²Hear diligently my speech;
and let this be your consolations.
³Suffer me, and I also will speak;
and after that I have spoken, mock
on.
⁴As for me, is my complaint of
man?
and why should I not be im-
patient?
⁵Mark me, and be astonished,
and lay your hand upon your
mouth.
⁶Even when I remember I am
troubled,
and horror taketh hold on my
flesh.
⁷Wherefore do the wicked live,
become old, yea, wax mighty in
power?
⁸Their seed is established with them
in their sight,
and their offspring before their
eyes.

⁹Their houses are safe from fear,
neither is the rod of God upon
them.
¹⁰Their bull gendereth, and faileth
not;
their cow calveth, and casteth not
her calf.
¹¹They send forth their little ones
like a flock,
and their children dance.
¹²They sing to the timbrel and
harp,
and rejoice at the sound of the
pipe.
¹³They spend their days in prosperity,
and in a moment they go down to
Sheol.
¹⁴Yet they said unto God, Depart
from us;
for we desire not the knowledge of
thy ways.
¹⁵What is the Almighty, that we
should serve him?

and what profit should we have,
if we pray unto him?

¹⁶Lo, their prosperity is not in their
hand:
the counsel of the wicked is far
from me.

¹⁷How oft is it that the lamp of the
wicked is put out?
that their calamity cometh upon
them?
that *God* distributeth sorrows in
his anger?

¹⁸that they are as stubble before
the wind,
and as chaff that the storm carrieth away?

¹⁹*Ye say*, God layeth up his iniquity
for his children.
Let him recompense it unto himself, that he may know it.

²⁰Let his own eyes see his destruction,
and let him drink of the wrath of
the Almighty.

²¹For what pleasure hath he in his
house after him,
when the number of his months is
cut off in the midst?

²²Shall any teach God knowledge?
seeing he judgeth those that are
high.

²³One dieth in his full strength,
being wholly at ease and
quiet:

²⁴his breasts are full of milk,
and the marrow of his bones is
moistened.

²⁵And another dieth in bitterness of
soul,
and never tasteth of good.

²⁶They lie down alike in the dust,
and the worm covereth them.

²⁷Behold, I know your thoughts,
and the devices which ye wrong-
fully imagine against me.

²⁸For ye say, Where is the house of
the prince?
and where is the tent wherein the
wicked dwelt?

²⁹Have ye not asked them that go
by the way?
and do ye not know their tokens?

³⁰That the evil man is spared in the
day of calamity?
that they are led away in the day
of wrath?

³¹Who shall declare his way to his
face?
and who shall repay him what he
hath done?

³²Yet shall he be borne to the grave,
and shall keep watch over the
tomb.

³³The clods of the valley shall be
sweet unto him,
and all men shall draw after him,
as there were innumerable before
him.

³⁴How then comfort ye me in vain,
seeing in your answers there remaineth only falsehood?

JOB was too much under the influence of his vision of God his
Vindicator for Zophar's angry words to touch him as they
would have earlier. Only his *mock on* (singular! 21: 3) shows
that the arrow of 20: 19 had not left him untouched. He asked
his friends to listen and so give him consolation (21: 2)—a touch
of sarcasm this—for he had something to lay before them that
would strike them dumb (v. 5).

The thought that lay hidden under the Why? of ch. 3, under
the glimpse of the universality of human suffering in ch. 7, which
for a moment was openly expressed in 9: 22ff., now comes out into
the open. It had been dropped while his friends' accusations had
driven him to self-vindication and to God for vindication. Now
that he knows that God will yet be on his side, he can face the

deeper cause of his agony, his doubt of that moral government of
the world on which all the theories of the Wise were based.

Job looks at the wicked, the *resha'im*, at Mr. Badman, who fears
neither man nor God, and has no respect for law, whether God's
or man's.   What he sees makes him deny all he was taught and
all his friends have been telling him.   Mr. Badman lives to a
prosperous old age, and his children flourish after him; when the
time comes for death it is a falling asleep: *They go down at last
without a struggle to the grave* (21: 13, Knox).   Though they flout
God (21: 14f.), there is no supernatural intervention in their lives:
Behold, is not their prosperity in their hands? (21: 16, R.S.V.).

To forestall his friends' angry interruption Job challenges them,
"How often do things turn out the way you say (vv. 17f.)?   Or,
if you are going to push the judgment off on his children (v. 19),
what does Mr. Badman care about that, once his life is run
(vv. 20f.)?"

Silenced for a moment, they let Job continue.   He maintains
that things are even worse than he has depicted.   Mr. Badman
goes down to the grave without knowing an evil hour: Mr. Good-
man dies without knowing a good hour, and yet there is the same
end for both (vv. 23–26).   In fact his friends' arguments pointed
to quite opposite conclusions to those they had drawn.   Any
traveller (v. 29) could tell them *that the wicked man is spared in
the day of calamity, that he is rescued in the day of wrath* (v. 30,
R.S.V.), and his tomb is honoured in days to come.   In fact, so
implies Job, he must obviously be a good man, if his friends'
theories and the aphorisms of the Wise are correct.

What shall we say to Job before Eliphaz explodes?   Is there
any truth in his charge?   That he exaggerates is obvious, but
under other circumstances he would probably have owned up to
this himself.

To begin with we must acknowledge that long before the time
of Job's friends down to our own the religious man has tended
to distort the facts.   God is the impartial pourer of His gifts on
godly and ungodly alike (Matt. 5: 45), and the great scourges of
nature have normally smitten godly and ungodly alike.   While
from Scripture, Church history and personal experience we can
find a goodly number of examples of God's judgment on the
wicked, we can as easily find at least as many examples of the
sufferings of the righteous.   More than that, the reverse is also
true.   The worst king of Judah, Manasseh, also reigned the longest.

Beside a Hitler and a Mussolini reaping the whirlwind in their deaths, we must place a Lenin and Stalin dying in their beds. Though "Yea, and all that would live godly in Christ Jesus shall suffer persecution" (II Tim. 3: 12) is a New Testament statement, "For Thy sake we are killed all the day long: we are accounted as sheep for the slaughter" (Psalm 44: 22, cf. Romans 8: 36) is equally true for the Old Testament, if we but read between the lines. When a crowded congregation breathes Hallelujah at some outstanding testimony of God's keeping, it is apt to forget the many who have gone to prison, and death with praise in their hearts to God. Lowell exaggerated, as Job did, when he wrote,

> Truth for ever on the scaffold,
> Wrong for ever on the throne,

but with his knowledge of the cross he could balance it, as Job could not, with,

> And, behind the dim unknown,
> Standeth God within the shadow,
> Keeping watch above His own.

When God's will is done and God's law is respected, the righteous are likely to prosper and the wicked to suffer. Indeed, wherever law is at all respected the righteous will profit from it. But since we know that the whole world, i.e. human society, lies in the evil one (I John 5: 19), we must expect that the moral government of God will often not be visible, and in place of prosperity the believer will have to say, "We know that in everything God works for good with those who love Him" (Rom. 8: 28, R.S.V.).

As the second round in the debate closes we find that the initiative has passed to Job. He is still wrestling with his problems, which we are beginning to see in their true proportions. His friends, however, are fighting desperately to salvage some part of their treasured ideas from the onslaught of this savage to whom nothing is sacred. It would have been well for them, if they had left then and there, but Eliphaz is not prepared to confess quite so easily that he has been defeated.

CHAPTER VII

ORTHODOXY CONFOUNDED

"THOU ART THE MAN!" (CH. 22)

THEN answered Eliphaz the Temanite, and said,

2Can a man be profitable unto God? surely he that is wise is profitable unto himself.

3Is it any pleasure to the Almighty, that thou art righteous? or is it gain *to him*, that thou makest thy ways perfect?

4Is it for thy fear *of him* that he reproveth thee, that he entereth with thee into judgement?

5Is not thy wickedness great? neither is there any end to thine iniquities.

6For thou hast taken pledges of thy brother for nought, and stripped the naked of their clothing.

7Thou hast not given water to the weary to drink, and thou hast withholden bread from the hungry.

8But as for the mighty man, he had the earth; and the honourable man, he dwelt in it.

9Thou hast sent widows away empty, and the arms of the fatherless have been broken.

10Therefore snares are round about thee, and sudden fear troubleth thee,

11Or darkness, that thou canst not see, and abundance of waters cover thee.

12Is not God in the height of heaven? and behold the height of the stars, how high they are!

13And thou sayest, What doth God know? can he judge through the thick darkness?

14Thick clouds are a covering to him, that he seeth not; and he walketh on the vault of heaven.

15Wilt thou keep the old way which wicked men have trodden?

16who were snatched away before their time, whose foundation was poured out as a stream:

17who said unto God, Depart from us; and, What can the Almighty do to us?

18Yet he filled their houses with good things; but the counsel of the wicked is far from me.

19The righteous see it, and are glad; and the innocent laugh them to scorn:

20*saying*, Surely they that did rise up against us are cut off, and the remnant of them the fire hath consumed.

21Acquaint now thyself with him, and be at peace: thereby good shall come unto thee.

22Receive, I pray thee, instruction from his mouth, and lay up his words in thine heart.

23If thou return to the Almighty, thou shalt be built up; if thou put away unrighteousness far from thy tents.

24And lay thou *thy* treasure in the dust,

and *the gold of* Ophir among the stones of the brooks;
²⁵and the Almighty shall be thy treasure,
and precious silver unto thee.
²⁶For then shalt thou delight thyself in the Almighty,
and shalt lift up thy face unto God.
²⁷Thou shalt make thy prayer unto him,
and he shall hear thee; and thou shalt pay thy vows.

²⁸Thou shalt also decree a thing, and it shall be established unto thee;
and light shall shine upon thy ways.
²⁹When they cast *thee* down, thou shalt say, *There is* lifting up;
and the humble person he shall save.
³⁰He shall deliver him that is innocent:
yea, he shall be delivered through the cleanness of thine hands.

WE have seen that Eliphaz the Temanite was at heart a good, kindly and God-fearing man. But Job had been dragging him remorsely to the cliff's edge and at last in his picture of Mr. Badman (ch. 21) had forced him to look down on a storm-tossed world in which there was no vestige of Divine rule and justice. In very terror Eliphaz turned on him.

Let us not be too hard on him. He was potentially the best of Job's friends, but the firm ground on which he thought he stood was essentially less secure than that of the others. Bildad relied on the consensus of human wisdom—if he had lived today, it would have been on some traditional scheme of Scripture interpretation or dogmatic theology—and Zophar on common-sense, but Elpihaz' rock was his own experience. Our experience of God may seem the most certain and comforting thing in life, but in the hour of crisis it may fail us completely, as Asaph discovered (Ps. 77: 6–9). Eliphaz was not the last in his position to panic, when his experience seemed to be contradicted.

Eliphaz begins by repeating the main thought of his dream (vv. 2–4, cf. 4: 17–20). When he had first told it, it might have seemed to the hearer as no more than one of those solemn experiences that colour and mould a man's life. Now we see that it had become a tyranny that held him as in a strait-jacket. Not merely Job but also God was to be understood in terms of the dream, and so Job had to become the chief of sinners and God the mere cold embodiment of an idea. This is the ultimate fate of all those who insist on interpreting God wholly in terms of their own experience.

Somewhat reassured by finding his feet once more on his familiar rock, Eliphaz turns in cold fury on the man who had made his universe shake for a moment. From the poor he had taken his outer garment (cf. Exod. 22: 26f., Deut. 24: 12f.) for a derisory loan (*for nought*, v. 6). Though he had been *mighty* and *honourable* (v. 8), he had ignored the needy (v. 7) and refused to help the widow and orphan in the hour of their greatest need (v. 9, cf. Exod. 22: 22ff.).

It might be profitable for us to pause in our reading and mentally to draw our own picture of Mr. Badman. It is bound to be different, for society has not only changed but also grown so much more complex, and the ties of the family group with its loyalties correspondingly weaker. But is our picture the true one? The sin above all others condemned by our Lord is sin against the weak—the sin against the Holy Spirit is an attitude of mind and heart to God and does not come into consideration here—for He said:

> It is impossible but that occasions of stumbling should come: but woe unto him, through whom they come! It were well for him, if a millstone were hanged about his neck, and he were thrown into the sea, rather than that he should cause one of these little ones to stumble (Luke 17: 1f.).

Love is the sign of life, lovelessness of death (I John 3: 14). So, provided we make allowances for the changes in society, the true Mr. Badman of today would bear close resemblance to Eliphaz' picture.

Eliphaz has one more shaft left to fire. He deliberately takes a phrase from Job's picture of Mr. Badman (21: 14f.) and applies it to Job (22: 12–17). Job is not merely bad, he IS Mr. Badman.

The typical modern atheist is the product of that intellectual pride of humanism that makes man the measure of all things and of the self-confidence of modern science. At his best there is something noble but pathetic about him. We have only to compare Psa. 23 with Henley's

> "Out of the night that covers me,
>   Black as the pit from pole to pole,
> I thank whatever gods may be
>   For my unconquerable soul"

to realize the vanity and emptiness of human pride.

But the atheist of the Old Testament is the fool (*nabal*) who says in his heart, "There is no God" (Psa. 10: 4, 14: 1, 53: 1). He crosses our path again and again in Scripture and in our daily lives. It is not that he denies the existence of God by word or intellectual argument; it is his life that denies it. He thinks that if there is a God He is not concerned with him (Psa. 10: 11, 73: 11), or even that God is like him in character (Psa. 50: 21). As a result the only check upon his behaviour is self-interest. Such a one, according to Eliphaz, is Job!

There is nothing vindictive about all this once Eliphaz has regained his equilibrium. Let Job but vindicate Eliphaz' experience and judgment, and he holds out to him in genuine warmth the riches of God's mercy (vv. 21–30) in language that reminds us of his earlier appeal in 5: 17–26. I am sure that, by the time he had finished, the hard feelings had evaporated, and that he was fully expecting Job to take his place on the penitent form. Once again we see how the self-centredness of the "good" man takes "Let God be found true, but every man a liar" (Rom. 3: 4) and makes it run "Let my understanding of God be found true, but every man that disagrees with it a liar."

"I Cannot Understand" (Ch. 23)

THEN Job answered and said,
²Even to-day is my complaint bitter:
his hand is heavier than my groaning.
³Oh that I knew where I might find him,
that I might come even to his seat!
⁴I would order my cause before him,
and fill my mouth with arguments.
⁵I would know the words which he would answer me,
and understand what he would say unto me.
⁶Would he contend with me in the greatness of his power?
Nay; but he would give heed unto me.
⁷There the upright might reason with him;
so should I be delivered for ever from my judge.
⁸Behold, I go forward, but he is not *there*;
and backward, but I cannot perceive him:

⁹on the left hand, when he doth work, but I cannot behold him:
he hideth himself on the right hand, that I cannot see him.
¹⁰But he knoweth the way that I take;
when he hath tried me, I shall come forth as gold.
¹¹My foot hath held fast to his steps;
his way have I kept, and turned not aside.
¹²I have not gone back from the commandment of his lips;
I have treasured up the words of his mouth more than my necessary food.
¹³But he is one, and who can turn him?
and what his soul desireth, even that he doeth.
¹⁴For he performeth that which is appointed for me:
and many such things are with him.
¹⁵Therefore am I troubled at his presence;
when I consider, I am afraid of him.

¹⁶For God hath made my heart faint,
and the Almighty hath troubled me:

¹⁷because I was not cut off before the darkness,
neither did he cover the thick darkness from my face.

I CAN see the ghost of a smile flit over Job's face marked with the scars of disease and suffering. At long last innuendoes and hints had come to an end and Job knew what they had been thinking all along, even though they might not have said it even to one another. As long as there seemed to be a shred of justification in the accusation, the desire for self-justification rose in his heart, but this nonsense could be ignored.

Eliphaz had capped Job's exaggeration about Mr. Badman with even greater exaggeration. This must have helped to restore Job's balance, and I get the impression that he had been quietly telling God that he knew that he had been drawing the long bow a trifle; but, for all that, he could not understand God's ways among men, for—and here he begins to speak aloud, to God, not to his friends—he could not understand God's ways with him.

The atmosphere and confidence of ch. 19 are still with us. There is no doubt in Job's mind that if he could only have a face-to-face talk with God he would be able to clear up the mystery. The progress of Job's thought is fascinating, but to understand it we must think of this chapter as a soliloquy with pauses from time to time. In vv. 2–7 it is not the old rebellious wish to argue out his case with God that we hear, but rather the sequel to 19: 27. The A.V. and R.V. mg. are correct as against R.V. text in v. 2, which we should, however, render with the R.S.V. (Moffatt essentially concurs):

Today also my complaint is bitter,
His hand is heavy in spite of my groaning.

Vindication after death is all very well, but the wronged heart of man yearns for it in this life. Let it be even in private, but *I should be acquitted for ever by my judge* (v. 7, R.S.V.).

Alas, there was no such finding of Him (vv. 8f.), but instead of this reducing Job to despair, as it did formerly, it only led him on spiritually. No longer do we get the strange picture of a duality in God, of a God who contradicts Himself (cf. 7: 8, 21; 16: 19). Now Job realized, even if only for a passing moment, that the mystery of darkness that had fallen on him was only God's refining fire (v. 10). Since in the days of his prosperity

Job had set himself to know God's will and to do it (vv. 11f.), he had no doubt as to the outcome.

In any case, he realized, the wish to find God was foolish, for *He is unchangeable* (v. 13, R.S.V., a translation that gives much the same sense as the emendation supported by most modern scholars, "He hath chosen"), and so all Job's arguments would be wasted. He must await the working out of God's will (v. 14); with that he sinks back temporarily into his misery (vv. 15ff.).

For those who from their childhood have known God only as seen in the face of Jesus Christ, it is hard to realize to what extent the Incarnation has made God more humanly comprehensible to us, and how, for this very reason, the Gospel is such a stumbling block to both Judaism and Islam. But this very comprehensibility constantly leads us into a hopelessly superficial outlook on life around us, and on God's ways with it.

There are not a few who assure us that it is comparatively easy to come to the throne of God and to talk things out with Him and so to obtain complete clarity on our own problems and often on those of others. Some claim to be able to do this by a correct use of the Scriptures, others by a technique of prayer or "listening," yet others by due attention to "the inner light." I do not want to seem to deny the strong element of truth in this, but it is a most serious exaggeration. Even our Lord on the cross cried out, "My God, My God, why . . .?" Though God graciously allows Himself to be found in measure by those who seek Him, He remains the God who hides Himself, and not until we see Him shall we know fully as we have been fully known.

So we find that today, as in the days of Job, while good men insist on the greatness of God and on the inscrutability of His sovereign purpose, they are convinced, for all that, that His purposes are easily discernible in the daily round of life, in spite of the fact that experience repeatedly denies their assertions. To affirm that "we know that in everything God works for good with those who love Him" (Rom. 8: 28, R.S.V.) is an expression of faith, not of understanding. To count it all joy, when we meet various trials (James 1: 2) is to recognize with joy God's working, but it does not imply knowledge of the extent or of the immediate purpose of the trial. In spite of the superficial optimism of our pundits, God does bring Himself glory by early death, ill-health, poverty, inability to use the gifts of God's own giving and the many other things which we are often assured should have at the

F

most a transient place in the Christian's life.   It is our failure to realize this that brings so many of God's afflicted ones to the verge of despair, and sometimes beyond it.

THE EVILS OF SOCIETY (CH. 24)

WHY are times not laid up by the Almighty?
and why do not they which know him see his days?

²There are that remove the land-marks;
they violently take away flocks, and feed them.

³They drive away the ass of the fatherless,
they take the widow's ox for a pledge.

⁴They turn the needy out of the way:
the poor of the earth hide themselves together.

⁵Behold, as wild asses in the desert they go forth to their work, seeking diligently for meat;
the wilderness *yieldeth* them food for their children.

⁶They cut their provender in the field;
and they glean the vintage of the wicked.

⁷They lie all night naked without clothing,
and have no covering in the cold.

⁸They are wet with the showers of the mountains,
and embrace the rock for want of a shelter.

⁹There are that pluck the fatherless from the breast,
and take a pledge of the poor:

¹⁰they go about naked without clothing,
and being an-hungred they carry the sheaves;

¹¹they make oil within the walls of these men;
they tread *their* winepresses, and suffer thirst.

¹²From out of the populous city men groan,
and the soul of the wounded crieth out:

yet God imputeth it not for folly.

¹³These are of them that rebel against the light;
they know not the ways thereof, nor abide in the paths thereof.

¹⁴The murderer riseth with the light, he killeth the poor and needy;
and in the night he is as a thief.

¹⁵The eye also of the adulterer waiteth for the twilight,
saying, No eye shall see me:
and he disguiseth his face.

¹⁶In the dark they dig through houses:
they shut themselves up in the daytime;
they know not the light.

¹⁷For the morning is to all of them as the shadow of death;
for they know the terrors of the shadow of death.

¹⁸*Ye say*, He is swift upon the face of the waters;
their portion is cursed in the earth:
he turneth not by the way of the vineyards.

¹⁹Drought and heat consume the snow waters:
so doth Sheol *those which* have sinned.

²⁰The womb shall forget him; the worm shall feed sweetly on him;
he shall be no more remembered:
and unrighteousness shall be broken as a tree.

²¹He devoureth the barren that beareth not;
and doeth not good to the widow.

²²Yet *God* by his power maketh the mighty to continue:
he riseth up, and no man is sure of life.

²³*God* giveth them to be in security, and they rest thereon;

and his eyes are upon their ways.
24They are exalted; yet a little while,
  and they are gone;
  yea, they are brought low, they
  are taken out of the way as all
  other,

and are cut off as the tops of the
  ears of corn.
25And if it be not so now, who will
  prove me a liar,
  and make my speech nothing
  worth?

ALREADY in our study of chs. 7 and 14 we saw how Job's
suffering gave him a truer picture of human life as a whole
than that possessed by his friends.   With the slackening of
tension brought by the rise of hope Job was able to look at the
suffering around him more objectively.   In answering Zophar the
second time (ch. 21) Job had merely challenged and denied his
friends' fundamental outlook on life.   Now he works out the
implications of his challenge.   He looks on life and cries out:

Why has not the Almighty sessions of set justice?
Why do His followers never see Him intervening? (24: 1,
  Moffatt).

Many scholars feel that this chapter is an anti-climax after the
very strong language of ch. 21 and suggest that Job did in fact
express himself so vigorously about the fate of the righteous that
some pious scribe felt compelled to replace what he considered
blasphemy by relatively harmless platitudes.   Quite apart from
the inherent objection to such a view, it is to ignore the change
in mood that set in in ch. 19, and also the background of the whole
book.   It is true that Job had become one of the great and
mighty, but the whole discussion is on the level of the Wise.
These were in ancient society, together with many of the priests,
the nearest approach to our modern middle class.   Except where
they dabbled in plots, or where the state went down in blood and
fire, they were more cushioned against sudden adversity than
others.

They were peculiarly prone to the besetting weakness of
the middle classes: an undue respect for the rich and powerful,
and a blind eye for the need and suffering of the poor.   This was
strengthened by a tendency we find throughout ancient society,
which is reflected in the Old Testament.

When John the Baptist wished to know of a certainty what he
had to think of Jesus, the supreme proof of His Messiahship was
"the poor have the gospel preached to them" (Matt. 11: 5).
Though we seldom recognize the fact, the Old Testament, quite
in keeping with its historic background, is concerned mainly with

the full citizen in Israel. The landless and broken man, the slave, and the hired servant, the harlot and the outcast, the bastard and the leper leave their mark on its pages, but it is seldom that the prophetic message is addressed to them, and often they had no place within the cultus of Israel.

It was not until the Son of God came in utter poverty, and, after having grown up in a place from which nothing good could be expected (John 1: 46) and having consorted with the outcast and the notorious sinner, became an outcast by being hanged on a tree (Deut. 21: 23), that the average man could even conceive that God was concerned with the outcast. By the educating work of the Holy Spirit during the inter-testamental period the Pharisees had come to realize clearly enough that riches were not a guide to whether a man enjoyed God's favour, but the hard words, "This multitude which knoweth not the law are accursed" (John 7: 49) show how little true understanding most of them had for the outcast. It was not until Jewry knew itself as an outcast in exile that there grew up in many hearts a truer understanding for the broken and despised.

But do not let us criticize the men of the Old Testament or the Pharisees too readily. Though it could doubtless have been said of all the early churches as it was said to the Christians in Corinth, "Ye see your calling, brethren, how that not many wise men after the flesh, not many mighty, not many noble are called" (1 Cor. 1: 26), yet already James (2: 1ff.) had to warn against undue deference to the rich. It has not been so much false doctrine or antinomianism that have been the great enemies of the Church in every period, but rather an undue respect for riches and intellect, which has made the poor and outcast feel strangers in what should have been their home. Though there have been repeated movements inside and outside the organized Church to alter this, they have always succumbed sooner or later to the prevailing atmosphere.

Job had shared the prevailing feelings of the Wise. Not until he became an outcast did he see his fellow outcasts as his fellow men rather than as objects of charity or condemnation. He now saw that the fate of the weak (vv. 2–4) was due to the evil character of the strong and not to the sin of those they oppressed; equally, the bitter life of the landless and wronged (vv. 5–12) could not be imputed to their fault. Yet for all that there was no sign of God's judgment (vv. 1, 12c.). Because his friends assumed that the outcasts must be suffering for their own sin, they entirely failed to realize that even if the fate of the wicked was what they described, it would mean no relief for those whom they had wronged the most deeply. It was just here that Job saw the clearest proof of a lack of Divine rule in the world, and we fail to see the problem at our peril. The fact that we cheerfully assign the great and evil leaders of Fascism and Communism and the conscienceless controllers of world finance to hell does not answer the problem of their victims, godly and godless alike.

From the victims of wrongdoing Job turns (vv. 13–17) to a type of wrongdoer who plays little part in the thinking of his friends, but who, for all that, does more real harm to individuals and society than does the *rasha'*, the arrogantly wicked man, *viz.* the thief who is prepared to murder in cold blood, and the adulterer prepared to break up homes to satisfy his lusts. They shun the light of day, unlike the *rasha'*, and so escape detection, while they undermine society. Note the R.S.V. rendering in v. 17b, *For they are friends with the terrors of deep darkness.* It is given to few to see sin where it really is. The sinner is all too often profoundly comfortable at church services, for the sins denounced there have little relevance to his own life. Apart from that, however, we should realize that the real threat to society comes not from those who serve more than half a lifetime of penal servitude or even meet their end on the scaffold, but from those who make their own desires their god, but are normally sufficiently astute to keep within the letter of the law, while achieving their purposes.

Apparently the R.V. mg. and R.S.V. give the only acceptable sense when they render v. 18, *Ye say, He is swift . . .*; vv. 18ff. must apparently represent the opinions of Job's friends. The meaning and text of v. 24 are far from clear, but in the context it must mean that while death overtakes the wicked it is only the common fate of all. With his survey of life completed Job challenges his friends to prove him wrong (v. 25). They do not really try, for they know that Job has laid his finger on the mystery of God's providential dealings with men.

CONFUSION (CHS. 25–27)

THEN answered Bildad the Shuhite, and said,

2Dominion and fear are with him; he maketh peace in his high places.

3Is there any number of his armies?
and upon whom doth not his light arise?

⁴How then can man be just before God?
or how can he be clean that is born of a woman?
⁵Behold, even the moon hath no brightness,
and the stars are not pure in his sight:
⁶how much less man, that is a worm!
and the son of man, which is a worm!

26. Then Job answered and said,
²How hast thou helped him that is without power!
how hast thou saved the arm that hath no strength!
³How hast thou counselled him that hath no wisdom,
and plentifully declared sound knowledge!
⁴To whom hast thou uttered words?
and whose spirit came forth from thee?
⁵The shades tremble
beneath the waters and the inhabitants thereof.
⁶Sheol is naked before him,
and Abaddon hath no covering.
⁷He stretcheth out the north over empty space,
and hangeth the earth upon nothing.
⁸He bindeth up the waters in his thick clouds;
and the cloud is not rent under them.
⁹He closeth in the face of his throne,
and spreadeth his cloud upon it.
¹⁰He hath described a boundary upon the face of the waters,
unto the confines of light and darkness.
¹¹The pillars of heaven tremble
and are astonished at his rebuke.
¹²He stilleth the sea with his power,
and by his understanding he smiteth through Rahab.
¹³By his spirit the heavens are garnished;
his hand hath pierced the swift serpent.

¹⁴Lo, these are but the outskirts of his ways:
and how small a whisper do we hear of him!
but the thunder of his power who can understand?

27. And Job again took up his parable and said,
²As God liveth, who hath taken away my right;
and the Almighty, who hath vexed my soul;
³all the while my breath is in me,
and the spirit of God is in my nostrils;
⁴surely my lips shall not speak unrighteousness,
neither shall my tongue utter deceit.
⁵God forbid that I should justify you:
till I die I will not put away mine integrity from me.
⁶My righteousness I hold fast, and will not let it go:
my heart shall not reproach *me* so long as I live.
⁷Let mine enemy be as the wicked,
and let him that riseth up against me be as the unrighteous.
⁸For what is the hope of the godless,
when God cutteth him off,
when God taketh away his soul?
⁹Will God hear his cry,
when trouble cometh upon him?
¹⁰Will he delight himself in the Almighty,
and call upon God at all times?
¹¹I will teach you concerning the hand of God;
that which is with the Almighty will I not conceal.
¹²Behold, all ye yourselves have seen it;
why then are ye become altogether vain?
¹³This is the portion of a wicked man with God,
and the heritage of oppressors, which they receive from the Almighty.
¹⁴If his children be multiplied, it is for the sword;

and his offspring shall not be satisfied with bread.

[15]Those that remain of him shall be buried in death,
and his widows shall make no lamentation.

[16]Though he heap up silver as the dust,
and prepare raiment as the clay;
[17]he may prepare it, but the just shall put it on,
and the innocent shall divide the silver.

[18]He buildeth his house as the moth,
and as a booth which the keeper maketh.

[19]He lieth down rich, but he shall not be gathered;
he openeth his eyes, and he is not.
[20]Terrors overtake him like waters;
a tempest stealeth him away in the night.
[21]The east wind carrieth him away, and he departeth;
and it sweepeth him out of his place.
[22]For *God* shall hurl at him, and not spare:
he would fain flee out of his hand.
[23]Men shall clap their hands at him,
and shall hiss him out of his place.

WE have already seen in ch. II that the text of this section is almost certainly in confusion and that part may well have been lost. This suits the position of the speakers well enough, for it mirrors their own confusion of mind. The obstinacy of his friends has gradually driven Job to a position he hates and does not really want to defend. His friends on the other hand can only maintain their traditional positions by shutting their eyes to facts and by repeating platitudes in a loud voice.

We need not hesitate to hear Bildad in ch. 25, though it may well be that ch. 26 belongs to him too. If Bildad were, like the writer of Ecclesiastes, taking up an agnostic position and claiming that God's ways are beyond man's understanding, his contrast of God's greatness (25: 2f.) with man's sinfulness and insignificance (25: 4ff.) would be valid. But he entirely overlooks that the argument that is intended to crush Job's impious views is equally effective against his own confident picture of God's moral rule as seen in the prosperity of the good and destruction of the wicked. One of the commonest fallacies that beset good men is the idea that because a theory is "edifying" it must be true.

It could be that Job replies with an even stronger affirmation of God's all-might and concludes with an affirmation of complete agnosticism (26: 14). Since, however, this would be an implicit retraction of his arguments of ch. 24, which is most unlikely, we would do well to base no arguments on ch. 26.

There is no doubt that it is Job we hear in 27: 2–5. The witness of his conscience is too strong for him to bow to his friends' affirmations of his sinfulness or of the all-might of God. The voice of God will yet prostrate him in humility and penitence, but the purely human measuring rods used by his friends merely drive him to even deeper anguish.

Unless we are to plead for a sustained note of sarcasm, of which there is no indication and which we could hardly justify in the setting, it seems impossible to ascribe 27: 7-23 to Job. The passage is an affirmation of all the three friends have been proclaiming and a flat contradiction of Job's own views. We shall probably do best to see Zophar speaking here, making dogmatism take the place of evidence and vehemence that of proof. It may be that Job's answer is lost, or more probably he looks on such statements as unworthy of being refuted again and deals with them by implication in his summing up (chs. 29–31).

So the third round ends in inevitable confusion, the confusion that must arise when orthodoxy turns its back on experience and creates a world to suit its theories, and when experience ignores revelation and seeks to make itself the measure of truth.

CHAPTER VIII

JOB SUMS UP

AN INTERLUDE IN PRAISE OF WISDOM (CH. 28)

So far as we were able to interpret ch. 27, we heard Job ending his answers to his friends with a fierce and passionate self-vindication:

As God liveth, who hath taken away my right,
  and the Almighty, who hath made my life bitter;
as long as my breath is in me,
  and the spirit of God is in my nostrils;
my lips shall not speak falsehood,
  neither shall my tongue utter deceit.
God forbid that I should justify you:
  till I die I will not put away my integrity from me.
My righteousness I hold fast, and will not let it go;
  my heart doth not reproach me for any of my days (27: 2–6).

Note how often "me" and "my" recur in these few verses.

Silence fell on the dunghill, broken only by the call of playing children and the hum of the nearby town. Along the horizon the first hint of thunderclouds showed, while Job's friends looked at one another in terrified anger, and the young man Elihu drew a little nearer.

For twenty-five chapters of thrust and counter-thrust we have heard all the wisdom of the schools and the dogmatism of experience break over Job, only to leave him more unconvinced than at the first and the wisdom of the Wise confounded. To break the tension, to turn our attention from the clash of passion, and to prepare us for God's intervention, the author now introduces a poem on Wisdom. It would seem to be completely false to picture ch. 28 as Job's own words; it would be completely out of character, and 29: 1 should act as a warning against the supposition. We should rather think of a curtain descending for a brief interval at the tensest point of the drama.

SURELY there is a mine for silver,
and a place for gold which they
refine.
[2]Iron is taken out of the earth,
and brass is molten out of the stone.
[3]*Man* setteth an end to darkness,
and searcheth out to the furthest
bound
the stones of thick darkness and
of the shadow of death.
[4]He breaketh open a shaft away
from where men sojourn;
they are forgotten of the foot *that
passeth by*;
they hang afar from men, they
swing to and fro.
[5]As for the earth, out of it cometh
bread:
and underneath it is turned up as
it were by fire.
[6]The stones thereof are the place of
sapphires,
and it hath dust of gold.
[7]That path no bird of prey knoweth,
neither hath the falcon's eye seen it:
[8]the proud beasts have not trodden
it,
nor hath the fierce lion passed
thereby.
[9]He putteth forth his hand upon the
flinty rock;
he overturneth the mountains by
the roots.
[10]He cutteth out channels among
the rocks;
and his eye seeth every precious
thing.
[11]He bindeth the streams that they
trickle not;
and the thing that is hid bringeth
he forth to light.
[12]But where shall wisdom be found?
and where is the place of understanding?
[13]Man knoweth not the price thereof;
neither is it found in the land of
the living.
[14]The deep saith, It is not in me:

and the sea saith, It is not with me.
[15]It cannot be gotten for gold,
neither shall silver be weighed for
the price thereof.
[16]It cannot be valued with the gold
of Ophir,
with the precious onyx, or the
sapphire.
[17]Gold and glass cannot equal it:
neither shall the exchange thereof
be jewels of fine gold.
[18]No mention shall be made of coral
or of crystal:
yea, the price of wisdom is above
rubies.
[19]The topaz of Ethiopia shall not
equal it,
neither shall it be valued with pure
gold.
[20]Whence then cometh wisdom?
and where is the place of understanding?
[21]Seeing it is hid from the eyes of all
living,
and kept close from the fowls of
the air.
[22]Abaddon and Death say,
We have heard a rumour thereof
with our ears.
[23]God understandeth the way thereof,
and he knoweth the place thereof.
[24]For he looketh to the ends of the
earth,
and seeth under the whole heaven;
[25]to make a weight for the wind;
yea, he meteth out the waters by
measure.
[26]When he made a decree for the rain,
and a way for the lightning of the
thunder:
[27]then did he see it, and declare it;
he established it, yea, and searched
it out.
[28]And unto man he said,
Behold the fear of the Lord, that
is wisdom;
and to depart from evil is understanding.

THE poem divides into three parts: (*a*) vv. 1–11.   The skill of
man in discovering the hidden riches of the earth (this portion
is almost unintelligible in the A.V.; the translators obviously

did not know what to make of it); (*b*) vv. 12–22, Wisdom can
neither be found nor purchased; (*c*) vv. 23–28, God is the possessor
of Wisdom.

In the first section we have a remarkable picture of mining
operations in the author's time. He is fascinated by the thought
of the miner deep underground, while corn grows far above him
on the surface (v. 5). and the passing traveller has no conception
of what is happening under his feet (v. 4). In his pursuit of these
hidden treasures neither difficulty nor danger daunts the spirit
of man.

When we turn to Wisdom, *man does not know the way to it, and
it is not found in the land of the living* (v. 13, R.S.V.). Neither in
the depths of the ocean (v. 14) nor in those of Sheol (v. 22) is its
home to be found. Even if we could find its abode, all the riches,
of the world could not buy it (vv. 15–19).

In poetic imagery God is pictured as knowing Wisdom's dwelling,
for the whole world is known to Him (v. 24). In fact He *saw* and
searched out Wisdom at the creation (vv. 26f.). *To man, He has
told this much, that wisdom is fearing the Lord; here lies discernment,
in refusing the evil path* (v. 28, Knox).

For the Wise this is a commonplace and self-evident (cf. Prov.
1: 7, 3: 7, 9: 10, 14: 16, 15: 33, 16: 6, Eccles. 12: 13), but sometimes we are very apt to forget the commonplace and self-evident.
Neither Job's friends nor Job had been particularly concerned
with *the fear of the Lord*. Self-vindication, the vindication of
orthodoxy, yes, but no one had laid "his hand upon his mouth"
(40: 2) and listened to what God had to say. In their zeal for
orthodoxy, for their conception of God, Job's friends had gone far
down the evil path, while they slandered him. Now the curtain
goes up on the second part of the drama, and we are to see whether
they can find true Wisdom in spite of their disastrous start.

Job's Concluding Monologue (Chs. 29–31)

Job had introduced the whole discussion by his great impassioned "Why?" in ch. 3. Now that his friends had been silenced,
he summed up the whole situation in a long and poignant soliloquy.
He can hardly be addressing his friends. Though the formal
notice of their default is not given till 32:1, it is clear that they
had been dragged out of their depth and broken on Job's stubborn
refusal to bow to authority. In the second half of the drama

they are reduced to little more than decorative pieces of the background, as they gnaw their fingers in impotent anger and then look on in growing amazement as Job reacts to God's voice, which they could not understand though they heard it. Though Job addresses God directly only in 30: 20–23, it seems clear that ultimately the whole of these chapters is a rehearsal for God's ears.

There is, however, more to be said. Both in 29: 1 and 27: 1 Job is said to take up his *mashal*. A.V. and R.V. render "his parable," on which the kindest comment would be that it is lacking in intelligence, for nothing farther from a parable could well be imagined than these two sections. R.S.V. and I.C.C. have "discourse," which, though rather pompous, is intelligible, though it is no translation of *mashal*. This is used of didactic poems, e.g. Pss. 49, 78, and so we may perhaps render "instruction." If Job's friends, and for that matter we, have ears to hear, they will learn both from Job's defiant challenge and from his solemn recital of his life how inadequate is their superficial judgment based merely on a strictly selective observation of God's ways with men.

THE MEMORY OF HAPPIER DAYS (CH. 29)

AND Job again took up his parable, and said,
²Oh that I were as in the months of old,
as in the days when God watched over me;
³when his lamp shined above my head,
and by his light I walked through darkness;
⁴as I was in the ripeness of my days,
when the friendship of God was upon my tent;
⁵when the Almighty was yet with me,
and my children were about me;
⁶when my steps were washed with butter,
and the rock poured me out rivers of oil!
⁷When I went forth to the gate unto the city,
when I prepared my seat in the broad place,

⁸the young men saw me and hid themselves,
and the aged rose up and stood;
⁹the princes refrained talking,
and laid their hand on their mouth;
¹⁰the voice of the nobles was hushed,
and their tongue cleaved to the roof of their mouth.
¹¹For when the ear heard *me*, then it blessed me;
and when the eye saw *me*, it gave witness unto me:
¹²because I delivered the poor that cried,
the fatherless also, that had none to help him.
¹³The blessing of him that was ready to perish came upon me:
and I caused the widow's heart to sing for joy.
¹⁴I put on righteousness, and it clothed me:
my justice was as a robe and a turban.

¹⁵I was eyes to the blind,
  and feet was I to the lame.
¹⁶I was a father to the needy:
  and the cause of him that I knew
  not I searched out.
¹⁷And I brake the jaws of the un-
  righteous,
  and plucked the prey out of his
  teeth.
¹⁸Then I said, I shall die in my
  nest,
  and I shall multiply my days as
  the sand:
¹⁹my root is spread out to the waters,
  and the dew lieth all night upon
  my branch:
²⁰my glory is fresh in me,
  and my bow is renewed in my
  hand.

²¹Unto me men gave ear, and waited,
  and kept silence for my counsel.
²²After my words they spake not
  again;
  and my speech dropped upon
  them.
²³And they waited for me as for the
  rain;
  and they opened their mouth wide
  as for the latter rain.
²⁴I smiled on them when they had
  no confidence;
  and the light of my countenance
  they cast not down.
²⁵I chose out their way, and sat *as*
  chief,
  and dwelt as a king in the army,
  as one that comforteth the mour-
  ners.

JOB began by sketching his former happiness and prosperity. It is most striking that it was his fellowship with God that stood out in his memory; all the rest was derived and received its meaning from this.

He thought of *the days of my ripeness* (v. 4, I.C.C.)—"my autumn days" (R.S.V.) is more literal but misses the point, as does "my prime" (Moffatt). Job did not think back, as do so many, to the dreams and illusive promises of youth and young manhood. By the grace of God Job's life had borne fruit, and he was thinking of this solid reality. God had guarded him (v. 2), He had given him His guidance (v. 3, *above my head*, R.V. mg., is obviously correct) and friendship (v. 4, *when the friendship of God was upon my tent*, R.S.V.); in brief, *the Almighty was . . . with me* (v. 5a).

This had had as its inevitable result family happiness (v. 5b), prosperity (v. 6) and respect (vv. 7–10). But since prosperity will always command superficial respect, Job stressed that there was genuine reason for it (vv. 11–17). Moffatt renders v. 14 interestingly: *I wore the robe of charity and kindness, my justice was a tunic and a turban.* The verse brings together righteousness (*tsedeq*) and justice (*mishpat*, more literally the verdict spoken). But righteousness in the Old Testament, when used of God, refers not merely to His doing right, but to His doing it in the right way with compassion and understanding. Since the earthly judge was God's representative, it was always hoped that he would reflect God's righteousness in his exercise of human righteousness. As

Moffatt has rightly understood it, Job not only held the scales of justice evenly, but also knew how to interpret the rigour of law with love to the oppressed and needy. He found that he became what he practised: *I clothed myself with righteousness, and it clothed itself with me* (v. 14, I.C.C.).

This the real Job, the same through and through, without contradiction between profession and practice, theology and life. Dare we blame him, if he expected that his old age would be the climax of his prime? He would die in the bosom of a happy family, *I shall die with my nestlings* (v. 18, I.C.C.; "among my brood," Moffatt)—in a ripe old age. Does not our own conception of God lead us to expect this, unless indeed the righteous man has become involved in a general catastrophe? Moreover catastrophe in old age is generally far harder to understand and bear.

THE MISERY OF THE PRESENT (CH. 30)

B<small>UT</small> now they that are younger
than I have me in derision,
whose fathers I disdained to set
with the dogs of my flock.
²Yea, the strength of their hands,
whereto should it profit me?
men in whom vigour is perished.
³They are gaunt with want and
famine;
they gnaw the dry ground, in the
gloom of wasteness and desolation.
⁴They pluck salt-wort by the
bushes;
and the roots of the broom *are* to
warm them.
⁵They are driven forth from the
midst *of men*;
they cry after them as after a thief.
⁶In the clefts of the valleys must
they dwell,
in holes of the earth and of the
rocks.
⁷Among the bushes they bray;
under the nettles they are gathered
together.
⁸*They are* children of fools, yea,
children of base men;
they were scourged out of the land.
⁹And now I am become their song,
yea, I am a byword unto them.
¹⁰They abhor me, they stand aloof
from me,
and spare not to spit in my face.
¹¹For he hath loosed my cord, and
afflicted me,
and they have cast off the bridle
before me.
¹²Upon my right hand rise the rabble;
they thrust aside my feet,
and they cast up against me their
ways of destruction.
¹³They break up my path,
they set forward my calamity,
even men that have no helper.
¹⁴As through a wide breach they
come:
in the midst of the ruin they roll
themselves *upon me*.
¹⁵Terrors are turned upon me,
they chase mine honour as the
wind;
and my welfare is passed away as a
cloud.
¹⁶And now my soul is poured out
within me;
days of affliction have taken hold
upon me.
¹⁷In the night season my bones are
pierced in me,
and the *pains* that gnaw me take
no rest.
¹⁸By *his* great force is my garment
disfigured:

it bindeth me about as the collar
of my coat.
¹⁹He hath cast me into the mire,
and I am become like dust and
ashes.
²⁰I cry unto thee, and thou dost not
answer me:
I stand up, and thou lookest at me.
²¹Thou art turned to be cruel to me:
with the might of thy hand thou
persecutest me.
²²Thou liftest me up to the wind,
thou causest me to ride *upon it*;
and thou dissolvest me in the
storm.
²³For I know that thou wilt bring
me to death,
and to the house appointed for all
living.
²⁴Surely against a ruinous heap he
will not put forth his hand;
though *it be* in his destruction, *one
may utter* a cry because of these
things.

²⁵Did not I weep for him that was in
trouble?
was not my soul grieved for the
needy?
²⁶When I looked for good, then evil
came;
and when I waited for light, there
came darkness.
²⁷My bowels boil, and rest not;
days of affliction are come upon
me.
²⁸I go mourning without the sun:
I stand up in the assembly, and cry
for help.
²⁹I am a brother to jackals,
and a companion to ostriches.
³⁰My skin is black, *and falleth* from
me,
and my bones are burned with
heat.
³¹Therefore is my harp *turned* to
mourning,
and my pipe into the voice of
them that weep.

THAT the respect paid to money lasts no longer than the money
is a constant theme in world literature. Job himself would
have expected no less, but he found that respect for true
merit does not outlive the prosperity either. Now that he was
weighing his sufferings more dispassionately, he felt that this was
the greatest evil of all.

Already when considering ch. 19 we saw that, when he found
his friends shared in his neighbours' and relatives' scorn and condemnation of him, it drove him to cry for vindication, a cry that
led him to trust in God as his Vindicator. How deeply this
attitude of scorn had hurt Job we are now allowed to see. In the
New Testament we find Paul proclaiming that we find the example
of our Lord supremely in the fact that He did not consider His
divine glory as a thing to be grasped and held on to, but that He
emptied Himself, taking the form of a slave (Phil. 2: 5–8), and a
slave has no honour.

It is hard enough to forgo the accidental and unmerited prestige
of birth, rank and wealth for Christ's sake. It becomes a heavier
price than many are prepared to pay when they see that true
attainments, nobility of character, and even the gifts of the Spirit
remain unrecognized, as often as not, by their fellow Christians.

The context of Paul's description of the apostles,

> Being reviled, we bless; being persecuted, we endure; being
> defamed, we intreat; we are made as the filth of the world, the
> offscouring of all things even until now (1 Cor. 4: 12f.),

is worth pondering. Indeed some of the language in 2 Cor.
10–13 reveals how deeply some of the dishonouring attacks made
by the Judaizers had hurt Paul.

In ch. 19 Job was moved by the failure of his nearest to support
him, now his thoughts are fixed on the baseness of some of the
scum of society who ventured to turn on him. Today we are
unfortunately all too familiar with the gutter press and the licence
given to muck-raking reporters to hound the man who is down.
In the far more rigid social structure of oriental society this was
only possible, if the whole of society had turned against Job.
What made the attack of the rabble all the more bitter was their
lack of gratitude, for it was just they whom he had helped all he
could (29: 15ff.).

There are those, e.g. Moffatt, Strahan, Peake, who find too great
a contrast between 30: 2–8 in their present setting and the sympathy of 24: 2–12 and especially of 31: 15; hence they move these
verses to ch. 24 (cf. Moffatt *ad loc.*), where they become part of
the description of the plight of the poor. The suggestion is very
attractive, but with our complete lack of knowledge about the
transmission of the book it should not be lightly accepted, even
though the theory is not impossible. There is, however, a more
likely explanation of the apparent contradiction. Job was a very
human man under intense stress, and there are many apparent
inconsistencies in his words. What is even more important is that
Job never fell into the Marxist fallacy of thinking that because
some of the proletariat—those "who have nothing to lose but
their chains"—are the victims of injustice and oppression they
all are. Job knew that some of them had reached the depths
because their character had taken them there.

It seems best to interpret v. 11a as a plural: *They have unstrung
me and undone me* (Moffatt). Then vv. 9–14 are a consistent
description how Job had been treated by base men; the behaviour
of others may be inferred from it. In vv. 15–19 Job looks inward.
The suggestion that he is thinking particularly of his illness is
most doubtful. As the italics suggest, the A.V. and R.V. transla-

tion of v. 18a is unjustified; we should render with R.V. mg., *By His great force is my garment disfigured*, or with R.S.V., *With violence it seizes my garment*. In fact, as we have seen before, his bodily state is merely the outward expression of far greater inner anguish, but it reminds him that men were only persecuting him whom God had first *cast into the mire* (v. 19).

So Job's heart turned once again in appeal to the inscrutable Deity, who seemed to have shut up the fountains of mercy (vv. 20–24), even though Job himself had been merciful (vv. 25f.). It seems likely that Knox has found the meaning of the difficult picture in v. 22: *Didst Thou exalt me, lift me so high in the air, only to hurl me down in ruin?* But there was no voice that answered, and so Job ended the picture of misery by describing his sufferings once again (vv. 26–31).

A closer examination of these verses will suggest once again that Job's disease played little part in his anguish. In v. 27 we have the description of intense emotional suffering; there is no suggestion here of fever; R.S.V., Knox and Moffatt all give the modern idiom by using *heart* instead of "bowels." His appeal in the assembly for help (v. 28) was doubtless because of the wrong that base men had done him. The first half of this verse should probably be rendered with Moffatt and Strahan, *I wail, with none to comfort me*. The meaning of vv. 29f. should be clear enough, when we remember that Job had been cast out of the city, and that his only home was the dunghill outside the gate, where he was exposed to all the powers of the elements.

If we have been tempted to judge Job harshly, it may be that we are being forced to modify our verdict. It had been the presence and blessing of God that had poured radiance on the past; it was the veiling of God's face that had turned the present into night.

With that deep subtle intuition that suffering brings in its train, Job began to sense that his problem must be the problem of many others. As Strahan has written on v. 31: "The parallel phrase 'my harp is turned to mourning' leads one simply to expect 'and my pipe to wailing,' which would leave us thinking of Job in his lonely sorrow. But the poet hears, and lets his reader hear, 'the voice of them that weep,' making Job speak here, as so often elsewhere, not as an individual, but in the name of all who ever shed a bitter tear."

"I Am Innocent!' (Ch. 31)

I MADE a covenant with mine eyes;
how then should I look upon a
maid?
²For what portion *should I have* of
God from above,
and what heritage of the Almighty
from on high?
³Is it not calamity to the unrighteous,
and disaster to the workers of
iniquity?
⁴Doth not he see my ways,
and number all my steps?
⁵If I have walked with vanity,
and my foot hath hasted to deceit;
⁶(let me be weighed in an even balance,
that God may know mine integrity;)
⁷if my step hath turned out of the
way,
and mine heart walked after mine
eyes,
and if any spot hath cleaved to
mine hands:
⁸then let me sow, and let another
eat:
yea, let the produce of my field be
rooted out.
⁹If mine heart have been enticed
unto a woman,
and I have laid wait at my neighbour's door:
¹⁰then let my wife grind unto
another,
and let others bow down upon
her.
¹¹For that were an heinous crime;
yea, it were an iniquity to be
punished by the judges:
¹²for it is a fire that consumeth unto
Destruction,
and would root out all mine increase.
¹³If I did despise the cause of my
manservant or of my maid-
servant,
when they contended with me:
¹⁴what then shall I do when God
riseth up?
and when he visiteth, what shall I
answer him?

¹⁵Did not he that made me in the
womb make him?
and did not one fashion us in the
womb?
¹⁶If I have withheld the poor from
their desire,
or have caused the eyes of the
widow to fail;
¹⁷or have eaten my morsel alone,
and the fatherless hath not eaten
thereof;
¹⁸(nay, from my youth he grew up
with me as with a father,
and I have been her guide from
my mother's womb;)
¹⁹if I have seen any perish for want
of clothing,
or that the needy had no covering;
²⁰if his loins have not blessed me,
and if he were not warmed with
the fleece of my sheep;
²¹if I have lifted up my hand against
the fatherless,
because I saw my help in the
gate:
²²then let my shoulder fall from the
shoulder blade,
and mine arm be broken from the
bone.
²³For calamity from God was a
terror to me,
and by reason of his excellency I
could do nothing.
²⁴If I have made gold my hope,
and have said to the fine gold,
Thou art my confidence;
²⁵if I rejoiced because my wealth
was great,
and because mine hand had gotten
much;
²⁶if I beheld the sun when it shined,
or the moon walking in brightness;
²⁷and my heart hath been secretly
enticed,
and my mouth hath kissed my
hand:
²⁸this also were an iniquity to be
punished by the judges:
for I should have lied to God that
is above.
²⁹If I rejoiced at the destruction of
him that hated me,

or lifted up myself when evil found him;

³⁰(yea, I suffered not my mouth to sin
by asking his life with a curse;)

³¹if the men of my tent said not,
Who can find one that hath not been satisfied with his flesh?

³²the stranger did not lodge in the street;
but I opened my doors to the traveller;

³³if like Adam I covered my transgressions,
by hiding mine iniquity in my bosom;

³⁴because I feared the great multitude,
and the contempt of families terrified me,
so that I kept silence, and went not out of the door—

³⁵Oh that I had one to hear me!

(lo, here is my signature, let the Almighty answer me;)
and the indictment which mine adversary hath written!

³⁶Surely I would carry it upon my shoulder;
I would bind it unto me as a crown.

³⁷I would declare unto him the number of my steps;
as a prince would I go near unto him.

³⁸If my land cry out against me,
and the furrows thereof weep together;

³⁹if I have eaten the fruits thereof without money,
or have caused the owners thereof to lose their life:

⁴⁰let thistles grow instead of wheat,
and cockle instead of barley.

The words of Job are ended.

IN 13: 13–22 Job had challenged God to argue things out with him in whatever way He wished. Now he stood up and solemnly took the role of the accused. If God would not show Himself, would not bring an accusation, then Job would none the less, according to the court procedure of the time, clear himself with a solemn oath, listing all the conceivable crimes that might be charged against him and calling for dreadful penalties to fall on him, if he were lying.

From one point of view this is the climax of the book. Broken though he may be and an outcast, forsaken by God and despised by man, he will yet clear himself before God and man. Some commentators seek to rearrange the text. While their result is doubtless tidier, I doubt that Job was feeling in a tidy mood. One rearrangement is, however, unavoidable. It is impossible to believe that vv. 38–40 stood originally in their present position, though we cannot suggest with certainty the point in the chapter from which they have been displaced.

Job began (vv. 1–4) by affirming that since he recognized God's knowledge of his life (v. 4) and His punishment of the wicked (v. 3), *I imposed a covenant on my eyes; how then could I [even] look on a virgin?* (v. 1, I.C.C.). In other words, he had brought even his wayward sight under control, and he would not permit it to beguile his thoughts even to the most venial of sins.

The first group of sins he denied are insincerity—*vanity*—and deceit (v. 5), the leaving of the path of God's law, the yielding to covetous wishes, and the staining of his hands with wrong (v. 7). The imprecation (v. 8) is an almost proverbial one (cf. Deut. 28: 30, 33).

From the general Job passed to the particular, from the venial to the gross. In v. 9 he denied the sin of adultery, which weakens the whole foundation of society. The hypercritical have suggested that in v. 10 Job called down punishment on his wife instead of on himself. But there was no greater indignity, no greater confession of impotence, than to be unable to prevent the forcible carrying away of one's wife. Where honour ranked above all else, this dishonour was worse than death. There follow (vv. 13–23) a number of sins against the weak and helpless (cf. Exod. 22: 21–24, 23: 9; Deut. 24: 17, 27: 19). The point is that the weak and helpless were considered to be particularly under God's protection, so to wrong them was to defy God. In v. 13 Job denied that he had ever *rejected* (R.S.V.) any claim of his slaves against him. The slave had few rights before the law, but he did not take advantage of this fact, for both he and his slaves were equally the wonderful work of God (v. 15). The whole modern tendency is to affirm the equality of men; Job on the other hand would have denied this as folly. He stresses that men with all their manifold differences are equally the creation of an all-wise God, and hence all deserve the same respect and justice, which are worth far more than any theoretical equality that so many cannot use to advantage.

From this principle comes the affirmation (vv. 16f., 19f.) that those from whom God had withheld the prosperity He had granted Job had always shared in Job's prosperity. Nor had he used his rank and money to influence the judges (v. 21b—*the gate* was the scene of public justice, cf. Ruth 4) and so permit him to show violence to and oppress *the perfect* or unoffending (this, and not "fatherless," based on a different division of the Hebrew consonants, seems to be correct in v. 21a, see Strahan, I.C.C., Moffatt, etc.).

Job next denied all idolatry, inner and outer, the worship of money (vv. 24f.) and the worship of nature (vv. 26f.). He affirmed that he had been forgiving and hospitable (vv. 31f.—the A.V. has strangely inverted the sense in v. 31b; Job's servants are portrayed as hyperbolically suggesting that all the world had been feasted at Job's table).   If even, like most men (v. 33 mg.—possibly "from men," R.S.V., Moffatt), he had simply and hypocritically hidden his faults out of fear of men, then——

But why should Job continue?   He had claimed a standard that many Christians could not honestly pretend to have attained *Oh that I had one* [i.e. God] *to hear me!   Here is my signature!* Job was picturing his protestations and imprecations not merely pronounced, but written down and solemnly signed.

Let the Almighty answer me!   Before the accusations could be made, Job had answered them and challenged God to find something else to charge him with.

Oh that I had the scroll of indictment which mine accuser hath
    written!
Surely I would carry it on my shoulder;
    I would bind it on me as a crown—

i.e. he would make it public property and consider it his highest honour, for it would become clear that God had nothing to charge him with.

I would give Him an account of all my steps;
    like a ruler of men I would approach Him.

And so the words of Job are ended.   His friends are speechless (32: 1), for he has shown himself greater than they had ever imagined.   Even if the book were to end here, Job's sufferings would not have been in vain.   God had "winnowed out his path" (Psa. 139: 3), and all unknowingly Job was re-echoing the divine word to Satan, *Hast thou considered My servant Job . . . a perfect and an upright man?*

CHAPTER IX

ELIHU

So these three men ceased to answer Job, because he was righteous in his own eyes. ²Then was kindled the wrath of Elihu the son of Barachel the Buzite, of the family of Ram: against Job was his wrath kindled, because he justified himself rather than God. ³Also against his three friends was his wrath kindled, because they had found no answer, and yet had condemned Job. ⁴Now Elihu had waited to speak unto Job, because they were elder than he. ⁵And when Elihu saw that there was no answer in the mouth of these three men, his wrath was kindled.

⁶And Elihu the son of Barachel the Buzite answered and said,
I am young, and ye are very old;
wherefore I held back, and durst not shew you mine opinion.
⁷I said, Days should speak,
and multitude of years should teach wisdom.
⁸But there is a spirit in man,
and the breath of the Almighty giveth them understanding.
⁹It is not the great that are wise,
nor the aged that understand judgement.
¹⁰Therefore I said, Hearken to me;
I also will shew mine opinion.
¹¹Behold, I waited for your words,
I listened for your reasons,
whilst ye searched out what to say.
¹²Yea, I attended unto you,
and behold, there was none that convinced Job,
or that answered his words, among you.
¹³Beware lest ye say, We have found wisdom;
God may vanquish him, not man:
¹⁴for he hath not directed his words against me;
neither will I answer him with your speeches.
¹⁵They are amazed, they answer no more:
they have not a word to say.
¹⁶And shall I wait, because they speak not,
because they stand still, and answer no more?
¹⁷I also will answer my part,
I also will shew mine opinion.
²⁸For I am full of words;
the spirit within me constraineth me.
¹⁹Behold, my belly is as wine which hath no vent;
like new wine-skins it is ready to burst.
²⁰I will speak, that I may be refreshed;
I will open my lips and answer.
²¹Let me not, I pray you, respect any man's person;
neither will I give flattering titles unto any man.
²²For I know not to give flattering titles;
else would my Maker soon take me away.

As Job's last impassioned words rang out, his friends looked at each other and nodded almost imperceptibly. Their task was finished: they had vindicated the wisdom of the Wise, but all in vain. With heavy hearts at the impenitence of their old friend they prepared to leave, when they were startled by a new voice vibrant with passion: *I am young in years, and you are aged; therefore I was timid and afraid to declare my opinion to you* (32: 6, R.S.V.).

Modern commentators and writers are agreed by a large majority that chs. 32–37, containing the speeches of Elihu, are a later interpolation, though a few would see in them an after-thought by the original author. It may be frankly admitted that, superficially at least, their arguments are strong. But we must remember that, though he has since changed his mind, the American scholar Pfeiffer could write, "These arguments did not seem convincing to the present writer in 1915,"* and they have only become valid to him now because he has found a new and doubtful interpretation for Elihu's views. In addition different scholars mutually contradict one another in the purpose they suggest for the interpolation. If the book is in any sense a drama, the non-mention of Elihu at an earlier stage can be reasonably explained. Had the reader been waiting all the time for Elihu's cue, he might have missed much of the drama and tension in the speeches of Job and his friends. Were it true, as so many (but not Pfeiffer) maintain, that Elihu adds virtually nothing to the debate, it is difficult to see why anyone should have troubled to interpolate him.

The introduction of Elihu in prose (32: 2–5) indicates that a new element is being introduced. He is given a brief genealogy, something that is lacking in the case of Job and his friends. As was stressed at the beginning of this study, Job and his friends are introduced, irrespective of whether they were of good family or not, as representatives of the Wise. Their position in society rested on their own merits, not on those of their fathers. Elihu, however, is introduced as a young aristocrat. He does not share in the vested interests of the Wise, and he begins by challenging their whole position:

> I said, 'Let days speak,
>   and many years teach wisdom.'
> But it is the spirit in a man,
>   the breath of the Almighty,
>   that makes him understand.
> It is not the old that are wise,
>   nor the aged that understand right (32: 7ff., R.S.V.).

---

* Pfeiffer: *Introduction to the Old Testament* (1948), p. 673.

The Wise were not godless men; their goal was the understanding of the divine rule of the world, that they might direct
their own and their pupils' footsteps accordingly. But they believed that provided God gave them the right start—for Eliphaz,
as we have seen, it was religious experience, for Bildad the voice
of tradition, for Zophar sound common sense—their own reason
was ample and would bring them to their goal. Elihu challenges
them with the claim that man needs the inspiration of the Spirit
for this—*Yet God inspires a man, 'tis the Almighty who breathes
knowledge into him* (32: 8, Moffatt).

Beyond a doubt Elihu stands on firmer ground than the three
friends. With one burning phrase he has laid bare the inner
weakness of those who have spoken before him. Human reason
cannot grasp the depths of God's work in heaven or on earth (cf.
28: 20–28), but the sequel is to show that Elihu's claim to inspiration is as shallow as the three friends' claim to divine Wisdom.

A hint as to the outcome is given us already in the prose introduction to Elihu: *Against Job was his wrath kindled, because he
justified himself rather than God* (32: 2), which Moffatt rightly
interprets, "for making himself out to be better than God."
Even more than in the arguments of Job's friends we find in Elihu
the inability to bring together God's sovereign rule and His loving
concern for the individual. As a result he has even less sympathy
and understanding for Job's "Why?" than the others, though of
course there is more excuse for him than for the older men.

We are apt to find in Elihu a noble, youthful indignation, with
which, in fact, 32: 3 does not credit him. If we retain the Hebrew
text, we must render it with I.C.C., *because they had found no
answer, and had not shown Job to be unrighteous.* It is, however,
more probable that the rabbinic tradition, which makes this verse
one of the *tiqqune sopherim* (corrections of the scribes), eighteen
passages deliberately changed to avoid objectionable expressions,
is correct. In that case Job has been substituted for God, and
the original form will have been, "because they had found no
answer, and so had condemned God." We can see that Elihu's
"inspiration" was merely a true realization that the friends were
lacking in something, but not a revelation of what that lack was.

In fact Elihu represents a phenomenon we constantly meet for
good in our church life. The self-satisfaction of an older generation finally drives young men to revolt. In practice they seldom
say much that is new and seldom say it well, but there are

almost invariably glimpses of valuable truth which the older generation had missed to its loss.

Much in Elihu's speeches is strongly reminiscent of Eliphaz and Bildad, but it does not seem that Zophar appealed to him. He was genuinely shocked by three features in Job's words and he deals with them in turn. This gives us a useful criterion for the division of his answer.

Elihu's First Answer (Ch. 33)

Howbeit, Job, I pray thee, hear my speech,
and hearken to all my words.

2 Behold now, I have opened my mouth,
my tongue hath spoken in my mouth.

3 My words *shall utter* the uprightness of my heart:
and that which my lips know they shall speak sincerely.

4 The spirit of God hath made me,
and the breath of the Almighty giveth me life.

5 If thou canst, answer thou me;
set *thy words* in order before me, stand forth.

6 Behold, I am toward God even as thou art:
I also am formed out of the clay.

7 Behold, my terror shall not make thee afraid,
neither shall my pressure be heavy upon thee.

8 Surely thou hast spoken in mine hearing,
and I have heard the voice of *thy* words, *saying,*

9 I am clean, without transgression;
I am innocent, neither is there iniquity in me:

10 Behold, he findeth occasions against me,
he counteth me for his enemy:

11 He putteth my feet in the stocks,
he marketh all my paths.

12 Behold, I will answer thee, in this thou art not just;
for God is greater than man.

13 Why dost thou strive against him,
for that he giveth not account of any of his matters?

14 For God speaketh once,
yea twice, *though man* regardeth it not.

15 In a dream, in a vision of the night,
when deep sleep falleth upon men,
in slumberings upon the bed;

16 then he openeth the ears of men,
and sealeth their instruction,

17 that he may withdraw man *from his* purpose,
and hide pride from man:

18 he keepeth back his soul from the pit,
and his life from perishing by the sword.

19 He is chastened also with pain upon his bed,
and with continual strife in his bones:

20 so that his life abhorreth bread,
and his soul dainty meat.

21 His flesh is consumed away, that it cannot be seen;
and his bones that were not seen stick out.

22 Yea, his soul draweth near unto the pit,
and his life to the destroyers.

23 If there be with him an angel,
an interpreter, one among a thousand,
to shew unto man what is right for him.

24 then he is gracious unto him, and saith,
Deliver him from going down to the pit,
I have found a ransom.

25 His flesh shall be fresher than a child's;
he returneth to the days of his youth:

²⁶He prayeth unto God, and he is favourable unto him; so that he seeth his face with joy: and he restoreth unto man his righteousness.
²⁷He singeth before men, and saith, I have sinned, and perverted that which was right, and it profited me not:
²⁸he hath redeemed my soul from going into the pit, and my life shall behold the light.

²⁹Lo, all these things doth God work, twice, *yea* thrice, with a man,
³⁰to bring back his soul from the pit, that he may be enlightened with the light of living.
³¹Mark well, O Job, hearken unto me: hold thy peace, and I will speak.
³²If thou hast anything to say, answer me: speak, for I desire to justify thee.
³³If not, hearken thou unto me: hold thy peace, and I will teach thee wisdom.

ELIHU turns first to Job's protestations of innocence (vv. 8–11). He prefaces his answer, however, with a rather disingenuous claim to be doing what Job had wanted all along. In 9: 32–35 and 13: 20–22, Job in his anguish had called on God to remove His heavy hand from him, so that he might be able to stand and answer Him. Elihu, catching the words but not the sense, offers himself as God's spokesman without the dread of God surrounding him. If the language of vv. 2–7 seems rather involved, it is because he is making oblique references to Job's own words. He had completely failed to see that Job's agony had driven him to the point where only the voice of God Himself would satisfy him. (It is to be noted that the A.V. in v. 6a is impossible and completely distorts the picture.)

For the quotations in v. 9 compare 9: 21, 10: 7, 16: 17, 23: 10–12 and 27: 5, 6. This has been the way of the heresy-hunter down the ages; expressions are snapped up out of their factual and emotional contexts, and balancing statements like 7: 21 and 13: 26 are conveniently forgotten. In vv. 10, 11 Elihu goes on to summarize some of Job's complaints against God (cf. 10: 13–17, 19: 6–12, 13: 24, 27). He is undoubtedly correct when he sums up, *Behold, in this you are not right* (v. 12, R.S.V.), but he immediately dodges the issue by adding, *For God is greater than man*, i.e. "the moral loftiness of God's nature made it impossible that He should act in the arbitrary, hostile manner charged against Him by Job" (Davidson, *ad loc.*).

It is repeatedly stressed in Scripture that the character of God is known from His words and acts. We know Him not merely from what He claims to be but even more from what He has done. Job has claimed to depict God's character from the way He has treated him, but he has yet to realize that to argue from human finiteness to divine infinity on the basis of part of one's own experience (Job conveniently forgot the experiences of his earlier life), with a few hand-picked facts thrown in as a make-weight, is a perilous process. But Elihu has embarked on a much more perilous path. He dismisses Job's explanation of his experience with an airy wave of his hand as being incompatible with his *a priori* concept of God and goes on to give a completely arbitrary explanation of it.

But let us be fair to Elihu. If Job's sufferings mean very little to him, it is because he is a young man and they lie outside his experience. Although he has been genuinely shocked by Job's words (cf. 34: 7ff.), it has been shock, not the personal hurt that Job's friends felt. His view of God's character and ways may be somewhat theoretical, but it is noble. Instead of thinking of punishment he sees God active in salvation. He did not deny that men were punished for their sins (cf. 36: 13f.), but in his thoughts punishment took second place to restoration. Job had himself had a glimpse of this truth on a higher level (23: 10); what marks out Elihu from Job's friends is that his explanation (vv. 14–28) does not establish a ratio between sin and suffering. Who knows? Had the others been as wise as Elihu, the whole discussion might have flowed in other channels.

Elihu seems to envisage two methods of divine warning. The former (vv. 14–20), strongly influenced by Eliphaz' words (4: 12–19), is that of the warning dream. The latter (vv. 21–28) is illness. He uses popular ideas of angels of death (*the destroyers*, v. 22) and angels of mercy (v. 23). The *if* (v. 23) does not express doubt: Elihu's whole point is that there are a thousand, i.e. very many, angels of mercy available. It is not clear whether the speaker in v. 24 is the angel or God; the latter seems more natural. The "ransom" (*kopher*) is probably to be understood metaphorically of that which covered the sick man's sin, i.e. his repentance. Elihu was no more an inspired theologian than were Job's friends.

ELIHU'S SECOND ANSWER (Ch. 34)

MOREOVER Elihu answered and said,

2Hear my words, ye wise men;
and give ear unto me, ye that have knowledge.
3For the ear trieth words,
as the palate tasteth meat.

4Let us choose for us that which is right:
let us know among ourselves what is good.
5For Job hath said, I am righteous,
and God hath taken away my right:

⁶notwithstanding my right I am *accounted* a liar;
my wound is incurable, *though I am* without transgression.

⁷What man is like Job,
who drinketh up scorning like water?

⁸which goeth in company with the workers of iniquity,
and walketh with wicked men.

⁹For he hath said, It profiteth a man nothing
that he should delight himself with God.

¹⁰Therefore hearken unto me, ye men of understanding:
far be it from God, that he should do wickedness;
and from the Almighty, that he should commit iniquity.

¹¹For the work of a man shall he render unto him,
and cause every man to find according to his ways.

¹²Yea, of a surety, God will not do wickedly,
neither will the Almighty pervert judgement.

¹³Who gave him a charge over the earth?
or who hath disposed the whole world?

¹⁴If he set his heart upon himself,
if he gather unto himself his spirit and his breath;

¹⁵all flesh shall perish together,
and man shall turn again unto dust.

¹⁶If now *thou hast* understanding, hear this:
hearken to the voice of my words.

¹⁷Shall even one that hateth right govern?
and wilt thou condemn him that is just *and* mighty?

¹⁸Is it *fit* to say to a king, *Thou art* vile?
or to nobles, *Ye are* wicked?

¹⁹*How much less to* him that respecteth not the persons of princes,
nor regardeth the rich more than the poor?
for they all are the work of his hands.

²⁰In a moment they die, even at midnight;

the people are shaken and pass away,
and the mighty are taken away without hand.

²¹For his eyes are upon the ways of a man,
and he seeth all his goings.

²²There is no darkness, nor shadow of death,
where the workers of iniquity may hide themselves.

²³For he needeth not further to consider a man,
that he should go before God in judgement.

²⁴He breaketh in pieces mighty men without inquisition,
and setteth others in their stead.

²⁵Therefore he taketh knowledge of their works;
and he overturneth them in the night, so that they are destroyed.

²⁶He striketh them as wicked men
in the open sight of others;

²⁷because they turned aside from following him,
and would not have regard to any of his ways:

²⁸so that they caused the cry of the poor to come unto him,
and he heard the cry of the afflicted.

²⁹When he giveth quietness, who then can condemn?
and when he hideth his face, who then can behold him?
whether *it be done* unto a nation, or unto a man, alike:

³⁰that the godless man reign not,
that there be none to ensnare the people.

³¹For hath any said unto God,
I have borne *chastisement*, I will not offend *any more*:

³²That which I see not teach thou me:
if I have done iniquity, I will do it no more?

³³Shall his recompence be as thou wilt, that thou refusest it?
for thou must choose, and not I:
therefore speak what thou knowest.

³⁴Men of understanding will say unto me,

yea, every wise man that heareth me:

³⁵Job speaketh without knowledge, and his words are without wisdom.

³⁶Would that Job were tried unto the end,

because of his answering like wicked men.

³⁷For he addeth rebellion unto his sin,

he clappeth his hands among us, and multiplieth his words against God.

JUST as his first answer had contained a deliberate allusion to Eliphaz' position, so his second takes up Bildad's attitude. He appeals to the consensus of the Wise (vv. 2, 34) as Bildad had to tradition (8: 8ff.).

In his first answer, for all his weakness, we saw Elihu at his best; here he is at his worst. There we obviously have his own reflections, here he is mouthing the shibboleths he has learnt from his childhood. He sets up a completely *a priori* picture of God's rule in the world. We have seen that one of the outstanding features of Job's spiritual progress was his learning to look on life in a new way and to see things that had been hidden from him and his friends by the blinkers of preconceived ideas. But for all we can gather from Elihu's words he might have been away at lunch when Job was describing the world as he had come to see it. We must not forget that in the setting of the book of Job it is not a question whether Elihu is right or not—obviously he is right, at least in large measure—but whether he contributes anything to the solution of Job's "Why?" Obviously he does not. Equally today the Christian who merely repeats theological truths will seldom meet the needs of those who, battered in life, are asking "Why?"

It would seem that Elihu, being a young man of rank and riches, had grown up with a vested interest in the maintenance of society as it was. He believed not only that "the powers that be are ordained of God" (Rom. 13: 1), but also that the powers that be must be good. As a result he was more shocked by Job's challenge to the accepted order than by his apparent denial of sinfulness. This goes far to account for the complete lack of sympathy for Job in this chapter.

Elihu's attitude is the worse because of its emptiness. However much we may refuse to follow Bildad in his appeal to tradition, we have the feeling that here is a learned man whose views have been carefully thought through and elaborated and who knows all the arguments. His tragedy is that he has become the prisoner of a theory. With Elihu we gain the impression that he has never thought of applying the theories he has learnt off by heart to life around him.

This is a constant danger in any church, where the theological manual threatens to displace the Bible as the text-book for the young.   It is always easier to teach the adolescent theology than the Bible.   The danger is that he will become as orthodox but as empty as Elihu shows himself in this chapter.

ELIHU'S THIRD ANSWER (CHS. 35–37)

MOREOVER Elihu answered and said,

2Thinkest thou this to be *thy* right, or sayest thou, My righteousness is more than God's,

3that thou sayest, What advantage will it be unto thee?

What profit shall I have, more than if I had sinned?

4I will answer thee, and the companions with thee.

5Look unto the heavens, and see; and behold the skies, which are higher than thou.

6If thou hast sinned, what doest thou against him?

and if thy transgressions be multiplied, what doest thou unto him?

7If thou be righteous, what givest thou him?

or what receiveth he of thine hand?

8Thy wickedness *may hurt* a man as thou art;

and thy righteousness *may profit* a son of man.

9By reason of the multitude of oppressions they cry out;

they cry for help by reason of the arm of the mighty.

10But none saith, Where is God my Maker,

who giveth songs in the night:

11who teacheth us more than the beasts of the earth,

and maketh us wiser than the fowls of heaven?

12There they cry, but none giveth answer,

because of the pride of evil men.

13Surely God will not hear vanity, neither will the Almighty regard it.

14How much less when thou sayest thou beholdest him not,

the cause is before him, and thou waitest for him!

15But now, because he hath not visited in his anger,

neither doth he greatly regard arrogance;

16therefore doth Job open his mouth in vanity;

he multiplieth words without knowledge.

36. Elihu also proceeded, and said,

2Suffer me a little, and I will shew thee:

for I have yet somewhat to say on God's behalf.

3I will fetch my knowledge from afar,

and will ascribe righteousness to my Maker.

4For truly my words are not false: one that is perfect in knowledge is with thee.

5Behold, God is mighty, and despiseth not any:

he is mighty in strength of understanding.

6He preserveth not the life of the wicked:

but giveth to the afflicted *their* right.

7He withdraweth not his eyes from the righteous:

but with kings upon the throne he setteth them for ever, and they are exalted.

8And if they be bound in fetters, and be taken in the cords of affliction;

9then he sheweth them their work,

and their transgressions, that they have behaved themselves proudly.
¹⁰He openeth also their ear to instruction,
and commandeth that they return from iniquity.
¹¹If they hearken and serve *him*,
they shall spend their days in prosperity,
and their years in pleasures.
¹²But if they hearken not, they shall perish by the sword,
and they shall die without knowledge.
¹³But they that are godless in heart lay up anger:
they cry not for help when he bindeth them.
¹⁴They die in youth,
and their life *perisheth* among the unclean.
¹⁵He delivereth the afflicted by his affliction,
and openeth their ear in oppression.
¹⁶Yea, he would have led thee away out of distress
into a broad place, where there is no straitness;
and that which is set on thy table should be full of fatness.
¹⁷But thou art full of the judgement of the wicked:
judgement and justice take hold *on thee*.
¹⁸Because there is wrath, beware lest thou be led away by *thy* sufficiency;
neither let the greatness of the ransom turn thee aside.
¹⁹Will thy riches suffice, *that thou be* not in distress,
or all the forces of *thy* strength?
²⁰Desire not the night,
when peoples are cut off in their place.
²¹Take heed, regard not iniquity:
for this hast thou chosen rather than affliction.
²²Behold, God doeth loftily in his power:
who is a teacher like unto him?
²³Who hath enjoined him his way?
or who can say, Thou hast wrought unrighteousness?

²⁴Remember that thou magnify his work,
whereof men have sung.
²⁵All men have looked thereon;
man beholdeth it afar off.
²⁶Behold, God is great, and we know him not;
the number of his years is unsearchable.
²⁷For he draweth up the drops of water,
which distil in rain from his vapour:
²⁸which the skies pour down
and drop upon man abundantly.
²⁹Yea, can any understand the spreadings of the clouds,
the thunderings of his pavilion?
³⁰Behold, he spreadeth his light around him;
and he covereth the bottom of the sea.
³¹For by these he judgeth the peoples;
he giveth meat in abundance.
³²He covereth his hands with the lighting;
and giveth it a charge that it strike the mark.
³³The noise thereof telleth concerning him,
the cattle also concerning *the storm* that cometh up.

37. At this also my heart trembleth,
and is moved out of its place.
²Hearken ye unto the noise of his voice,
and the sound that goeth out of his mouth.
³He sendeth it forth under the whole heaven,
and his lightning unto the ends of the earth.
⁴After it a voice roareth;
he thundereth with the voice of his majesty:
and he stayeth them not when his voice is heard.
⁵God thundereth marvellously with his voice;
great things doeth he, which we cannot comprehend.
⁶For he saith to the snow, Fall thou on the earth;

likewise to the shower of rain,
and to the showers of his mighty
rain.
[7]He sealeth up the hand of every
man;
that all men whom he hath made
may know *it*.
[8]Then the beasts go into coverts,
and remain in their dens.
[9]Out of the chamber *of the south*
cometh the storm:
and cold out of the north.
[10]By the breath of God ice is given:
and the breadth of the waters is
straitened.
[11]Yea, he ladeth the thick cloud
with moisture;
he spreadeth abroad the cloud of
his lightning:
[12]and it is turned round about by
his guidance,
that they may do whatsoever he
commandeth them
upon the face of the habitable
world:
[13]whether it be for correction, or for
his land,
or for mercy, that he cause it to
come.
[14]Hearken unto this, O Job:
stand still, and consider the wondrous works of God.
[15]Dost thou know how God layeth
his charge upon them,
and causeth the lightning of his
cloud to shine?

[16]Dost thou know the balancings of
the clouds,
the wondrous works of him which
is perfect in knowledge?
[17]Thou whose garments are
warm,
when the earth is still by reason of
the south *wind*,
[18]canst thou with him spread out
the sky,
which is strong as a molten mir-
ror?
[19]Teach us what we shall say unto
him;
for we cannot order *our speech* by
reason of darkness.
[20]Shall it be told him that I would
speak?
or should a man wish that he were
swallowed up?
[21]And now men cannot look on the
light when it is bright in the
skies:
when the wind has passed, and
cleanseth them.
[22]Out of the north cometh golden
splendour:
God hath upon him terrible
majesty.
[23]The Almighty, we cannot find him
out; he is excellent in power:
and in judgement and plenteous
justice he will not afflict.
[24]Men do therefore fear him:
he regardeth not any that are wise
of heart.

As Elihu saw it, Job had not merely made baseless claims for himself and denied God's righteous rule of the world; he had also denied that there was any profit in serving God (35: 3, cf. 9: 22f., 30f., 21: 15, 24: 1), though it is questionable whether Job had ever intended his words to be so understood.

When Karl Marx declared that religion was opium for the people and that all promises of blessing for the keeping of the moral law were only means for making the proletariat satisfied with their chains, he put his finger on an all-too-frequent misuse of religion. All too often some subtle shift of emphasis has brought the official Church on to the side of the dominant classes. In Job's day the virtual equation of poverty and sin, not unknown in the Victorian age, was most comforting to the rich and powerful.

We do not doubt that Elihu was genuinely shocked by the suggestion that God would not reward those who served him, but equally
certainly the shock was increased by the uneasy knowledge that,
if Job was right, he would have to reconsider his whole outlook
on the world. This probably explains the rather malicious reference to Job's *companions* (35: 4), literally "friends"; he is probably thinking of the rich, careless wicked whom Job had so
graphically described, e.g. 21: 14f., and he suggests that Job for
all his outward godliness was at heart one of them.

In the earlier part of his answer (35: 5–9) Elihu takes up and
expands Eliphaz' aphorism in 22: 2–4, but what was just within
the bounds of truth in the mouth of the older man becomes a
travesty of Scriptural truth as it is exaggerated by the younger.
But it is clear that he does not really believe his own picture of
God, for the one who gives "songs in the night" (35: 10f.) is not
the transcendent Deity, unmoved by the acts of His creation,
whom he had earlier depicted. We need not be surprised or distressed by this. There is little hope for the young man with a
fully co-ordinated theology; he is only a copy-cat or a poll-parrot.
True enough, Elihu was teaching when he should have been
learning, but he shows enough good for us to hope great things
for him.

He goes on to reveal this dichotemy in thought by expanding
in 36: 2–12 his thought of the drawing and teaching of God in
suffering. He goes so far as to call it a *ransom* (36: 18), presum-
ably in the sense that it will be accepted as such by God, if the
sinner bows under it and accepts it (cf. 33: 24). Even though
Elihu is as convinced as Job's friends that Job is a great sinner—
not, as with them, because of the greatness of his sufferings, but
because of the evil of his words—the R.V. translation of 36: 18f.,
is so wildly inappropriate to Job's position that we should
probably follow the R.S.V. rendering of a very difficult passage:

Beware lest wrath entice you into scoffing;
    and let not the greatness of the ransom turn you aside.
Will your cry avail to keep you from distress,
    or all the force of your strength?

For a moment Elihu strikes true Scriptural balance: *Behold, God
doeth loftily in His power: who is a teacher like unto Him?* (36. 22).
Then, however, he turns again to his concept of God All-Sovereign,
above the finding out and understanding of men (36: 26—37: 24).

H

It may well be that he was stung to the quick by a look of amusement on the faces of Job's friends. After all, with all his self-assurance he had ended up very much where they had and with even less result. He had not even stung Job into answering. So he launches out into a description of the wonders of God in nature to cover his confusion. But though he uses many words, and at times strikes genuinely poetic notes, he does not really add anything to what Job himself had said, viz. 9: 4–10; 12: 13–25, and perhaps 26: 6–14.

Is it too much to think that, as he describes the greatness of God, Elihu gradually realizes that he has rushed into a subject far too great for him? As his voice tails off there is no need for anyone to answer him; he has realized that after all righteous emotion need not be inspiration.

CHAPTER X

GOD REPLIES TO JOB

The Thunderstorm (38: 1)

> THEN the LORD answered Job out
> of the whirlwind, and said . . .

ELIHU'S many and brave words tailed out feebly with a final thrust both at Job and his friends: *The Almighty . . . regardeth not any that are wise of heart* (37: 24), which the R.S.V. interprets correctly as "wise in their own conceit." This is essentially a repetition of his challenge to the Wise in 32: 7–10.

While he had been speaking, the storm clouds had covered the sky and blotted out the sun. It is quite possible that the distant thunder had coloured Elihu's third answer, cf. 36: 29 – 37: 5. Now the full thunder-roll was heard overhead, and the gloom was lit up by the lightning's flash. For the men crouching in fear on the dunghill it seemed as though God had at last bestirred Himself to punish Job's blasphemies. They edged still further away from him, lest they be consumed with him. But as they glanced fearfully at him, instead of a look of fear and despair on Job's face they saw a joyous, humble awe. The Almighty had come to him, clothed in all the dread majesty of nature, but He had come and was speaking to Him!

The how of God's direct speaking should little concern us. Too many have heard the voice of God in thunder or in a still small voice for us to doubt that He speaks even in our days to men. But he who hears that voice has little time or wish to think of how it may be coming to him. In Job's case his friends almost certainly found themselves in the same position as Paul's travelling companions, "hearing the sound, but beholding no man" (Acts 9: 7, R.V. mg.), while for Job the storm became the voice of God speaking clearly to him.

God passes over the words of Elihu in silence (for it is merely a curiosity of interpretation to apply, *Who is this that darkeneth counsel by words without knowledge* to him) and this is seen by many as proof positive that Elihu's words are a later addition, But He equally passes over the words of Job's friends in silence, even though there is an almost parenthetical mention of them later (42: 7). God does not intervene to sum up and decide the debate; He speaks because behind all the multitude of words Job has been trying to storm the gates of heaven, and at last He has pity on His sorely tried servant and answers him.

THE ALL-MIGHT OF GOD

If we look away from some special passage like 19: 25ff., God's answer to Job is the best known portion of the book. Our familiarity with it helps to hide from us how entirely unexpected it is—but then we so seldom read through the book. It would seem as though God wishes by sledge-hammer blow after sledge-hammer blow to break down His already broken servant to nothing. In blazing poetry all the gamut of nature's wonders is passed before Job's eyes, but nothing is said about his agonized Why? But is all this as irrelevant as it seems?

To understand God aright we must remember that chs. 38–41 are ultimately only a repetition, more detailed and on a poetically much higher level, of what has already been said by Elihu (36: 22 – 37: 24) and by Job himself (9: 4–14, 12: 13–25 and perhaps 26: 4–14), and their thought underlies much that his friends have declared, e.g. Bildad in 25: 2–6. If we could accept Stevenson's view and completely separate the prose introduction and conclusion from the verse drama, then we could see in these chapters God's condemnation of Job's foolish words and an affirmation on a *higher level* of the views of his friends. But we are not entitled to do this, and in their setting, cf. 42:7, God's words are ultimately a vindication of Job and a condemnation of his friends.

In Rom. 1: 18–23 Paul described the reaction of man when faced by the all-might of God as seen in His creation. We in our spiritual superiority are apt to say,

> "The heathen in his blindness
> Bows down to wood and stone,"

and fail to realize that we too find means of coming to terms with God's all-might, which save us from taking it too seriously. There is a reverent freedom with God which is one of the noblest fruits of sonship, but there is also an irreverent freedom which is one of the worst weeds in the Christian's garden.

The Rabbinic Jew never for a moment doubted that the giving of the Law at Sinai was an even greater act of grace than the bringing up of Israel out of Egypt, of which it was a logical sequel. But he was profoundly convinced that once God had given it, the consensus of religious men's opinions about the Law established God's will for the individual and people. God had in measure abdicated His freedom of action by His giving of the Law.

In the Church the theologian has tended to take the place of the casuist. We have always recognized that in the incarnation, crucifixion and resurrection of the Son of God we have the supreme evidence of God's grace, but we have all too often believed that we have the right, and even the duty, to make our understanding of these events the measure by which we judge the acceptability of other men to God. It matters not how much of the fruit of the Spirit may be seen in them, if they will not or cannot say Shibboleth, we lay the command of silence upon them, or even thrust them from our midst as unclean.

This is only one of the ways in which we claim to be able to control God. The attitude of the various characters in *Job* may well suggest other ways in which we too are guilty.

For Job's friends the contemplation of God's all-might produced merely a comforting conviction that it provided that immutability which served as a firm foundation for their theories about life. They remind me of the many modern scientists—I am thinking of men who claim to believe in God—who base their denial of all miracle precisely on the wonder of God's creating. They wish to limit Him by that portion of His power and work that they are able to grasp.

For Elihu the all-might of God was a handy weapon to smite Job's presumption with. As we read 36: 22 – 37: 24, we never get the impression that the wonders of nature which he describes so eloquently have ever created humility in him. He may say, *At this also my heart trembleth, and is moved out of its place* (37: 1), but if there was any outward sign of it, it was the conventional one of the actor.

Even Job did not take God's power really seriously. Paul explains that it is revealed in nature, that men might glorify Him as God and give thanks (Rom. 1: 21). With Job we feel, as with his friends, that it is little more than a handy weapon in controversy; it was an intellectual concept to be appealed to in case of need, not the foundation of all his living. As a result, when Job faces it more seriously from time to time, in his discussion, it drives him to distraction rather than leading him on to confidence.

When God spoke out of the thunderstorm, intellectual conviction become a vital reality. It broke Job down, but it also brought him peace. A God, greater than Job had ever pictured Him, was deigning to speak to His sorely tried servant, and that sufficed.

The Casting Out of Fear

I am convinced, though, that we can go further. All the motives given hitherto for Job's anguish are doubtless valid, but behind them all lay a deeper cause we must now consider. We have already said of Job, "He finds that the firm moorings of his life have vanished, that the ship of his life is adrift on the dark ocean, without chart, without light, being carried he knows not where." God is now speaking to deeper need, to the hidden fear, hardly realized by Job and certainly unconfessed, that there might be somewhere where the writ of God did not run, where God was not all-sovereign.

Are we not all like Job in this respect? In his *Nineteen Eighty-Four* George Orwell makes his inquisitor, O'Brien, say to the hero, "You asked me once what was in Room 101. I told you that you knew the answer already. Everyone knows it. The thing that is in Room 101 is the worst thing in the world . . . The worst thing in the world varies from individual to individual. It may be burial alive, or death by fire, or by drowning, or by impalement, or fifty other deaths. There are cases where it is some quite trivial thing, not even fatal."

How true this is! Deep down in each one of us, unconfessed, and perhaps not even realized, there lies a fear, a fear that just here God's power is inadequate to triumph. Strangely enough it is all too often "some quite trivial thing." It is these deep, hidden fears that are the cause of so much disappointment in the Christian life, that give the lie to so much talk on sanctification and victory. It is only when we grasp the unique combination of love and power in the manger, the cross and the empty tomb that we can say with life as well as with lip, "We know that in everything God works for good with those who love Him" (Rom. 8: 28,

R.S.V.), and we experience the truth of the word, "Perfect love casteth out fear" (I John 4: 18).

This probably explains why God's answer to Job is such a fascinating combination of the great and the small. God's power is not affected by the scale it has to work on; the infinitely great and the microscopically small are equally under His control.

GOD'S ANSWER (CHS. 38–41)

2WHO is this that darkeneth counsel
by words without knowledge?
3Gird up now thy loins like a man;
for I will demand of thee, and declare thou unto me.
4Where wast thou when I laid the foundations of the earth?
declare, if thou hast understanding.
5Who determined the measures thereof, if thou knowest?
or who stretched the line upon it?
6Whereupon were the foundations thereof fastened?
or who laid the corner stone thereof;
7when the morning stars sang together,
and all the sons of God shouted for joy?
8Or *who* shut up the sea with doors, when it brake forth,
and issued out of the womb;
9when I made the cloud the garment thereof,
and thick darkness a swaddling band for it,
10and prescribed for it my boundary, and set bars and doors,
11and said, Hitherto shalt thou come, but no further;
and here shall thy proud waves be stayed?
12Hast thou commanded the morning since thy days *began*,
and caused the dayspring to know its place;
13that it might take hold of the ends of the earth,
and the wicked be shaken out of it?
14It is changed as clay under the seal;

and *all things* stand forth as a garment:
15and from the wicked their light is withholden,
and the high arm is broken.
16Hast thou entered into the springs of the sea?
or hast thou walked in the recesses of the deep?
17Have the gates of death been revealed unto thee?
or hast thou seen the gates of the shadow of death?
18Hast thou comprehended the breadth of the earth?
declare, if thou knowest it all.
19Where is the way to the dwelling of light,
and as for darkness, where is the place thereof;
20that thou shouldest take it to the bound thereof,
and that thou shouldest discern the paths to the house thereof?
21*Doubtless*, thou knowest, for thou was then born,
and the number of thy days is great!
22Hast thou entered the treasuries of the snow,
or hast thou seen the treasuries of the hail,
23which I have reserved against the time of trouble,
against the day of battle and war?
24Which is the way *to the place where* the light is parted,
or the east wind scattered upon the earth?
25Who hath cleft a channel for the waterflood,
or a way for the lightning of the thunder;

²⁶to cause it to rain on a land where
no man is;
on the wilderness, wherein there is
no man;
²⁷to satisfy the waste and desolate
ground;
and to cause the tender grass to
spring forth?
²⁸Hath the rain a father?
or who hath begotten the drops of
dew?
²⁹Out of whose womb came the ice?
and the hoary frost of heaven,
who hath given it?
³⁰The waters are hidden as *with* stone,
and the face of the deep is frozen.
³¹Canst thou bind the cluster of the
Pleiades,
or loose the bands of Orion?
³²Canst thou lead forth the signs of
the Zodiac in their season?
or canst thou guide the Bear with
her train?
³³Knowest thou the ordinances of
the heavens?
canst thou establish the dominion
thereof in the earth?
³⁴Canst thou lift up thy voice to the
clouds,
that abundance of waters may
cover thee?
³⁵Canst thou send forth lightnings,
that they may go,
and say unto thee, Here we are?
³⁶Who hath put wisdom in the dark
clouds?
or who hath given understanding
to the meteor?
³⁷Who can number the clouds by
wisdom?
or who can pour out the bottles of
heaven,
³⁸when the dust runneth into a mass,
and the clods cleave fast together?

³⁹Wilt thou hunt the prey for the
lioness?
or satisfy the appetite of the young
lions,
⁴⁰when they couch in their dens,
and abide in the covert to lie in
wait?

⁴¹Who provideth for the raven his
food,

when his young ones cry unto God,
and wander for lack of meat?

39. Knowest thou the time when
the wild goats of the rock bring
forth?
canst thou mark when the hinds
do calve?
²Canst thou number the months
that they fulfil?
or knowest thou the time when
they bring forth?
³They bow themselves, they bring
forth their young,
they cast out their sorrows.
⁴Their young ones are in good lik-
ing, they grow up in the open
field;
they go forth, and return not
again.

⁵Who hath sent out the wild ass
free?
or who hath loosed the bands of
the wild ass?
⁶whose house I have made the
wilderness,
and the salt land his dwelling
place.
⁷He scorneth the tumult of the city,
neither heareth he the shoutings of
the driver.
⁸The range of the mountains is his
pasture,
and he searcheth after every green
thing.

⁹Will the wild-ox be content to
serve thee?
or will he abide by thy crib?
¹⁰Canst thou bind the wild-ox with
his band in the furrow?
or will he harrow the valleys after
thee?
¹¹Wilt thou trust him, because his
strength is great?
or wilt thou leave to him thy
labour?
¹²Wilt thou confide in him, that he
will bring home thy seed,
and gather *the corn of* thy thresh-
ingfloor?

¹³The wing of the ostrich rejoiceth:
are her pinions and feathers
kindly?

¹⁴For she leaveth her eggs on the earth,
and warmeth them in the dust,
¹⁵and forgetteth that the foot may crush them,
or that the wild beast may trample them.
¹⁶She dealeth hardly with her young ones, as if they were not hers:
though her labour be in vain, *she is* without fear;
¹⁷because God hath deprived her of wisdom,
neither hath he imparted to her understanding.
¹⁸What time she lifteth up herself on high,
she scorneth the horse and his rider.

¹⁹Hast thou given the horse *his* might?
hast thou clothed his neck with the quivering mane?
²⁰Hast thou made him to leap as a locust?
the glory of his snorting is terrible.
²¹He paweth in the valley, and rejoiceth in his strength:
he goeth out to meet the armed men.
²²He mocketh at fear, and is not dismayed;
neither turneth he back from the sword.
²³The quiver rattleth upon him,
the flashing spear and the javelin.
²⁴He swalloweth the ground with fierceness and rage;
neither believeth he that it is the voice of the trumpet.
²⁵As oft as the trumpet *soundeth* he saith, Aha!
and he smelleth the battle afar off,
the thunder of the captains, and the shouting.

²⁶Doth the hawk soar by thy wisdom,
and stretch her wings toward the south?
²⁷Doth the eagle mount up at thy command,
and make her nest on high?

She dwelleth on the rock, and hath her lodging *there*,
upon the crag of the rock, and the strong hold.
²⁹From thence she spieth out the prey;
her eyes behold it afar off.
³⁰Her young ones also suck up blood:
and where the slain are, there is she.

40. Moreover the LORD answered Job, and said,
²Shall he that cavilleth contend with the Almighty?
he that argueth with God, let him answer it.
³Then Job answered the LORD, and said,
⁴Behold, I am of small account;
what shall I answer thee?
I lay mine hand upon my mouth.
⁵Once have I spoken, and I will not answer;
yea twice, but I will proceed no further.

⁶Then the LORD answered Job out of the whirlwind, and said,
⁷Gird up thy lions now like a man:
I will demand of thee, and declare thou unto me.
⁸Wilt thou even disannul my judgement?
wilt thou condemn me, that thou mayest be justified?
⁹Or hast thou an arm like God?
and canst thou thunder with a voice like him?
¹⁰Deck thyself now with excellency and dignity;
and array thyself with honour and majesty.
¹¹Pour forth the overflowings of thine anger:
and look upon every one that is proud, and abase him.
¹²Look on every one that is proud, *and* bring him low;
and tread down the wicked where they stand.
¹³Hide them in the dust together;
bind their faces in the hidden *place*.
¹⁴Then will I also confess of thee

that thine own right hand can save thee.

¹⁵Behold now behemoth, which I made with thee;
he eateth grass as an ox.
¹⁶Lo now, his strength is in his loins,
and his force is in the muscles of his belly.
¹⁷He moveth his tail like a cedar:
the sinews of his thighs are knit together.
¹⁸His bones are *as* tubes of brass;
his limbs are like bars of iron.
¹⁹He is the chief of the ways of God:
he *only* that made him can make his sword to approach *unto him.*
²⁰Surely the mountains bring him forth food;
where all the beasts of the field do play.
²¹He lieth under the lotus trees,
in the covert of the reed, and the fen.
²²The lotus trees cover him with their shadow;
the willows of the brook compass him about.
²³Behold, if a river overflow, he trembleth not:
he is confident, though Jordan swell even to his mouth.
²⁴Shall any take him when he is on the watch,
or pierce through his nose with a snare?

41. Canst thou draw out leviathan with a fish hook?
or press down his tongue with a cord?
²Canst thou put a rope of rushes into his nose?
or pierce his jaw through with a spike?
³Will he make many supplications unto thee?
or will he speak soft words unto thee?
⁴Will he make a covenant with thee,
that thou shouldest take him for a servant for ever?
⁵Wilt thou play with him as with a bird?

or wilt thou bind him for thy maidens?
⁶Shall the bands of *fishermen* make traffic of him?
shall they part him among the merchants?
⁷Canst thou fill his skin with barbed irons,
or his head with fish spears?
⁸Lay thine hand upon him;
remember the battle, and do so no more.
⁹Behold, the hope of him is in vain:
shall not one be cast down even at the sight of him?
¹⁰None is so fierce that he dare stir him up:
who then is he that can stand before me?
¹¹Who hath first given unto me,
that I should repay him?
whatsoever is under the whole heaven is mine.
¹²I will not keep silence concerning his limbs,
nor his mighty strength, nor his comely proportion.
¹³Who can strip off his outer garment?
who shall come within his double bridle?
¹⁴Who can open the doors of his face?
round about his teeth is terror.
¹⁵*His* strong scales are *his* pride,
shut up together *as with* a close seal.
¹⁶One is so near to another,
that no air can come between them.
¹⁷They are joined one to another;
they stick together, that they cannot be sundered.
¹⁸His neesings flash forth light,
and his eyes are like the eyelids of the morning.
¹⁹Out of his mouth go burning torches,
and sparks of fire leap forth.
²⁰Out of his nostrils a smoke goeth,
as of a seething pot and *burning* rushes.
²¹His breath kindleth coals,
and a flame goeth forth from his mouth.

²²In his neck abideth strength,
and terror danceth before him.
²³The flakes of his flesh are joined
together:
they are firm upon him; they cannot be moved.
²⁴His heart is as firm as a stone;
yea, firm as the nether mill-
stone.
²⁵When he raiseth himself up, the
mighty are afraid:
by reason of consternation they
are beside themselves.
²⁶If one lay at him with the sword,
it cannot avail;
nor the spear, the dart, nor the
pointed shaft.
²⁷He counteth iron as straw,
and brass as rotten wood.
²⁸The arrow cannot make him
flee:
slingstones are turned with him
into stubble.
²⁹Clubs are counted as stubble:
he laugheth at the rushing of the
javelin.
³⁰His underparts are *like* sharp
potsherds:
he spreadeth *as it were* a threshing
wain upon the mire.
³¹He maketh the deep to boil like a
pot:
he maketh the sea like ointment.
³²He maketh a path to shine after
him;
one would think the deep to be
hoary.
³³Upon earth there is not his like,
that is made without fear.
³⁴He beholdeth everything that is
high:
he is king over all the sons of pride.

God's answer to Job has by some been grievously mis-
interpreted as a catalogue of scientific marvels beyond
man's understanding, and as a revelation of scientific truth
that would be discovered only in the nineteenth or twentieth
century of our era. Nothing could be further from the truth.
God is here speaking to Job in terms of Job's knowledge and
ignorance. It is quite secondary whether modern man has or
has not found the answers to God's questions. As for the fore-
shadowings of modern scientific knowledge, they are, at least in
part, due more to "eisegesis," i.e. reading in, than to exegesis.

Today God will speak to the thinking man in terms of *his*
knowledge and ignorance. God's creation challenges the modern
biologist or atomic physicist with other questions than those Job
could not answer, but the challenge is as real.

It is typical of the attitude of the Bible that God's questions
virtually restrict themselves to this world, in which man was
placed as God's vice-regent (Gen. 1: 28, Psa. 8: 6). God scarcely
asks Job about the mysteries of the stars on their silent way, but
He faces him with everyday things of this world, in which man
is ever tempted to speak Himself free of his Creator.

God's questions range from the earth's mysterious uniqueness
in the universe (38: 4–7) and the power that maintains the nightly
star pattern, as typified in the Pleiades, Orion and the signs
of the Zodiac, constant in its risings and settings (38: 31f) to

the forces that maintain animal life in all its manifestations
(38: 39 – 39: 4). He is questioned as to his control of the sea,
of light and darkness, of snow, hail and ice (38: 8–30). These last
refer especially to those sudden and incalculable phenoma of
nature which overthrow all the power and forethought of man.
Though man has been set to rule the animal creation, there are
those he cannot control: the wild ass (39: 5–8), the wild ox
(39: 9–12)—the A.V. "unicorn" is as imaginary as the beast itself
—the ostrich (39: 13–18), the hawk and the eagle (39: 26–30), or
if he does control, it may be at his peril as with the horse
(39: 19–25).

When Job confesses himself overwhelmed and convinced
(40: 3ff), God points out the futility and negative character of
his criticism of the moral rule of the world (40: 11ff), for he cannot
do anything about it himself. Then God turns to the apparently
irrational in His creation. This has already been indicated in
passing in 38: 25ff—why should it rain, where it does no one any
good? Now Job is asked to consider a couple of God's "jokes."
However much our cold northern minds may resent the fact, the
Bible is an oriental book and from time to time bursts out into
the glorious, unrestrained hyperbole of the east. Though they
may not appear so to our minds—are we perhaps the losers
thereby?—behemoth (40: 15–24) is the hippopotamus and
leviathan (41: 1–34) the crocodile. Quite candidly I prefer this
hyperbole to the perverted ingenuity that can see a prophecy of
the modern battleship in the description of leviathan.

Why did God make the hippopotamus and the crocodile? If
you have never asked yourself this question, you may find a
couple of hours spent in the nearest zoo a worth-while investment.
Some of us have a private list to which we have added a few
more names. The Wise prided themselves that they were basing
their views on the fundamental rationality of God's acts. So
God faces Job with a couple of His "jokes," and Job repents in
dust and ashes (42: 6).

CHAPTER XI

JOB'S VINDICATION

THEN Job answered the LORD, and said,

2I know that thou canst do all things,
and that no purpose of thine can be restrained.

3Who is this that hideth counsel without knowledge?
therefore have I uttered that which I understood not,
things too wonderful for me, which I knew not.

4Hear, I beseech thee, and I will speak;
I will demand of thee, and declare thou unto me.

5I had heard of thee by the hearing of the ear;
but now mine eye seeth thee.

6wherefore I loathe my words,
and repent in dust and ashes.

7And it was so, that after the LORD had spoken these words unto Job, the LORD said to Eliphaz the Temanite, My wrath is kindled against thee, and against thy two friends: for ye have not spoken of me the thing that is right, as my servant Job hath. 8Now therefore, take unto you seven bullocks and seven rams, and go to my servant Job, and offer up for yourselves a burnt offering; and my servant Job shall pray for you; for him will I accept, that I deal not with you after your folly; for ye have not spoken of me the thing that is right, as my servant Job hath. 9So Eliphaz the Temanite and Bildad the Shuhite and Zophar the Naamathite went, and did according as the LORD commanded them: and the LORD accepted Job. 10And the LORD turned the captivity of Job, when he prayed for his friends: and the LORD gave Job twice as much as he had before. 11Then came there unto him all his brethren, and all his sisters, and all they that had been of his acquaintance before, and did eat bread with him in his house: and they bemoaned him, and comforted him concerning all the evil that the LORD had brought upon him: every man also gave him a piece of money, and every one a ring of gold. 12So the LORD blessed the latter end of Job more than his beginning: and he had fourteen thousand sheep, and six thousand camels, and a thousand yoke of oxen, and a thousand she-asses. 13He had also seven sons and three daughters. 14And he called the name of the first, Jemimah; and the name of the second, Keziah; and the name of the third, Keren-happuch. 15And in all the land were no women found so fair as the daughters of Job: and their father gave them inheritance among their brethren. 16And after this Job lived an hundred and forty years, and saw his sons, and his sons' sons, *even* four generations. 17So Job died, being old and full of days.

SATAN had said to God, *Doth Job fear God for nought? ... Put forth Thine hand now, and touch all that he hath, and he will renounce Thee to Thy face* (1: 9, 11). Job has lost all, but he has found God and is content. Even without the knowledge of

God's love that comes from Golgotha, he finds Him more than suf-
ficent.   The passionate cry for vindication has been forgotten, for it
matters not what men may say, if he knows that his fellowship
with God has been restored.

The vindication of some of God's saints must wait until they
stand before His throne.   Job, however, has been more than just
an individual who through suffering and loss has reached the bliss
of communion with God; he is also an object lesson from whom
generations to come were to learn a lesson of God's dealings with
men.   He had therefore to be vindicated there and then.   This
comes in two stages.

Though nothing we have said about Job's friends has been too
hard, they were for all that men who sought the truth, even though
they wished to force it into their own moulds, so God was able
to speak to them.   It is not surprising that He chose Eliphaz
(42: 7), for his distorting medium was more pardonable than that
of the others.   That it was Job who had to pray for them (42: 8),
Job the outcast, the chief of sinners, was something that could
break down even the common-sense of Zophar.   It was clear that
only a man accepted by God and righteousness in His sight could
mediate for his fellow-men.

But what of Job's fellow-townsmen, the fickle mob that had
thrust him out of their town as unclean and accursed, when the
hand of Satan was upon him?   There was only one answer they
could understand, the only answer the mob will ever understand,
and so *the Lord restored the fortunes of Job . . . and gave Job twice
as much as he had before* (v. 10, R.S.V.).   Success and prosperity
form the language the world understands, so they all flocked back
to the man they had abandoned in the hour of his bitterest need
(42: 11).   He might well have thanked God that they had treated
him as they did, for had he known their comfort and care in his
adversity, he might never have been thrown back on God and
so have learnt to know Him in this new way.

Many have found the end of *Job* disappointing, for, so they say,
it is ultimately no more than a vindication of the views that Job's
friends had put forward all along.   Even if this were true, what
of it?   It is not Job's words, but Job, who is vindicated; it is
Job's friends rather than their theology that stands condemned.
The force of 42: 7 is that however foolishly he may have said it,
Job was looking for a God big enough to comprehend his experience.   On the other hand, however wisely they may have put

it into words, his friends were upholding a God small enough to conform to their theories. Could the discussion have been carried on in a vacuum, it may well be that we should have been forced to adjudge the friends victors. But theological discussions cannot be carried on in a vacuum. We have to bow before what God has done in history, before what He has done to individual men and women, of whom Job was but one.

But that is not all. God is never concerned that some insist on misunderstanding Him. There was only one way in which He could vindicate Job that the mob would understand. If that way could be interpreted as a vindication of the theory that Job had by his sufferings so signally refuted, that was of no concern to God. Experience shows us that sinful man is happily capable of misinterpreting anything that God has said and done.

The doubling of all Job's possessions was intended to show that there was nothing fortuitous about it all; his contemporaries had to be made to acknowledge that God's hand was at work. Only his children were not doubled (42: 13). In the hour of Job's greatest desperation he had been driven to the hope of life beyond the grave. Now God says Amen to it. All earthly things are transient, and so his lost possessions could not be restored, but only replaced and doubled. But by giving him only ten new children God assured him that he would yet meet those he had lost beyond the grave.